SPIRITIST
JOURNEY

IN 1862

SPIRITIST
JOURNEY

IN 1862

© Copyright 2019 by the United States Spiritist Council

Unless otherwise indicated, all Scriptures are from the Holy Bible, English Standard Version, copyright © 2001 by Crossway Bibles, a publishing ministry of Good News Publishers. Used by permission. All rights reserved.

ISBN: 978-1948109147
LCCN: 2019947008
Translation: Helton Mattar Monteiro
Proofreading: Jussara Korngold
Book design: Helton Mattar Monteiro
Cover design: HML

International data for cataloging in publication (CIP)

K1829sj Kardec, Allan
        Spiritist journey in 1862/ Allan Kardec. Translator: Helton Mattar Monteiro. – New York: United States Spiritist Council, 2019.
        136 pp.; 21.59 cm.

        Original title: Voyage spirite en 1862 (Paris: Ledoyen, 1862).
ISBN: 978-1948109147

        Includes bibliography.

        1. Spiritism. 2. Spiritualism. 3. France. 4. 19th century. I. Title
        LCCN: 2019947008   DDC 133.9   UDC 133.9

1st edition, 1st print – July 2019

All rights reserved to
United States Spiritist Council
http://www.spiritist.us – info@spiritist.us
Book portal: https://is.gd/ussf1

Manufactured in the United States of America

ALLAN KARDEC

SPIRITIST JOURNEY

IN 1862

UNITED STATES
SPIRITIST FEDERATION
NEW YORK
2019

About the Book

When Allan Kardec set out for his historical journey of 1862, not even he could have foreseen the immense growth of Spiritism in France, inaugurated with the publication of *The Spirits' Book* in Paris only five years earlier. In a time when there was no radio, nor any other means of mass communication other than the printed word, that span was remarkable by any standards. Offering some rare glimpses into the Codifier's way of thinking, this book covers some practical aspects of nascent Spiritism, while keenly narrating its quiet triumph against formidable odds and opposition.

USSF

CONTENTS

GENERAL
IMPRESSIONS

My first Spiritist tour, which took place in 1860, was confined to Lyon and some towns on my route. The following year I added Bordeaux to my itinerary, and this year, in addition to these two main cities, during a seven-week journey covering 693 leagues (i.e., 2079 miles), I visited about twenty localities and attended more than fifty meetings. My aim is not to give an anecdotal account of my excursion; I have collected all the episodes which, perhaps one day, will not be without interest, because they will be part of history. Yet today I will be content to summarize the observations I have made on the state of Spiritism, and to bring to everybody's attention the instructions I have given at different centers. I know that true Spiritists desire it, and I am more keen to satisfy them than those who seek only a pastime. Besides, in this chronicle, my self-esteem would too often be involved, which is a preponderant factor for me to abstain from it. That is also the main reason that prevents me from publishing the many speeches addressed to my person, which I nonetheless keep as precious memories. What I could not fail to mention without being guilty of ingratitude was the kind and sympathetic welcome I received, which alone would have sufficed to make up for my hardships. I am particularly indebted to the Spiritists of Provins, Troyes, Sens, Lyon, Avignon, Montpellier, Cette, Toulouse, Marmande, Albi, Sainte-Gemme, Bordeaux, Royan, Meschers-sur-Garonne, Marennes, Saint-Pierre d'Oléron, Rochefort, St. Jean d'Angély, Angoulême, Tours and Orleans; and all those who were not discouraged by the prospect of a journey of ten and twenty leagues to join me in the towns where I stopped. Such a reception could really have made me proud, had I not considered that these demonstrations were addressed much less to me personally, than to Spiritism, of which they can see the merit, since without it I myself would be nothing, and not worthy of any attention from them.

The first result I have seen is the immense progress of Spiritist beliefs. A single fact will serve to give an idea of it. During my first trip to Lyon in 1860, there were at most a few hundred adherents; the following year there were already five to six thousand; and this year it is impossible to count them. Yet one can, without exaggeration, estimate their number as twenty-five to thirty thousand individuals. In Bordeaux, last year, there were not a thousand; however, in the space of a year their number has increased tenfold. This is a constant occurrence that no one can deny. Another fact that I have been able to note, and which is remarkable, is

FRANCE

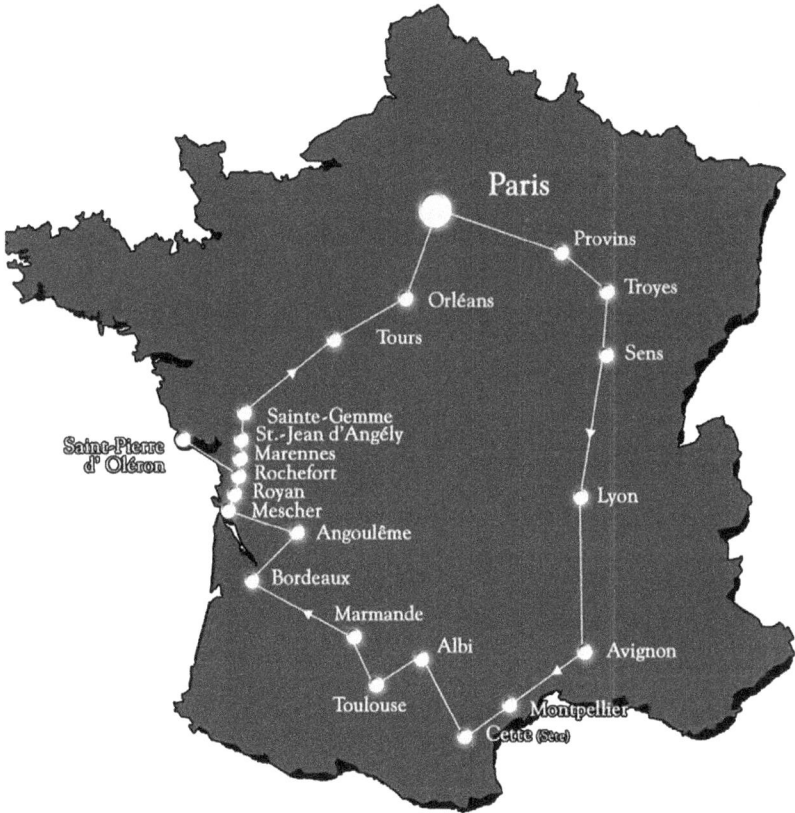

Journey itinerary for 1862 *

(*) *Map based on the one published by the French branch of the ISC.*

that in a host of localities where Spiritism used to be unknown, it has now penetrated, thanks to hostile preachings that made it known and aroused the curiosity to learn about it. Then, as it was found to be rational, it conquered more adherents. I could mention, among others, a small town in the department of Indre-et-Loire, where, only six months ago at most, no one had ever heard of it, when it came to a local priest the idea of rushing into the pulpit against what he falsely and awkwardly called the religion of the 19th century and the worship of Satan. Surprised, the population wanted to know what it was: books were brought, and today the adherents have formed a Spiritist center there. It is true that the spirits were right when they told me a few years ago that my adversaries would serve my cause despite themselves. It is common ground that everywhere the spread of Spiritism has occurred because of attacks. Now, for an idea to propagate in this way, it must be pleasing and found to be more rational than that which is opposed to it. One of the results of my trip was to see with my own eyes what I already knew from my correspondence.

It is true, however, to say that this ascending course has been far from uniform. If there are some regions where the idea of Spiritism seems to sprout from the moment it is sown, there are others where it penetrates less easily, for local reasons, such as the character of the inhabitants, and especially due to the nature of their occupations. Spiritists are found sparsely and in isolation; but here, as elsewhere, these are the roots that sooner or later will have offshoots, as has been seen in numerous centers nowadays. Everywhere the Spiritist idea begins to flourish in the more enlightened, average class of people; nowhere does it begin in lesser, rather ignorant categories. From the middle group it spreads up and down the social scale. Today, several cities have Spiritist meetings almost entirely composed of attorneys, members of the judiciary, and civil servants. The aristocracy also supplies its contingent of adherents, but so far they are content to be sympathetic to the cause and meet very little – at least in France. Meetings of this kind are to be found mostly in Spain, Russia, Austria, and Poland, where Spiritism has enlightened representatives of the highest social ranks.

Perhaps even more importantly than the number that has emerged from my observations, is the serious approach with which they regard Spiritism. Everywhere I seek, I can say with alacrity, I encounter its philosophical, moral and instructive sides highlighted. Nowhere have I seen it treated as a subject of amusement, nor has the pursuit of experiments been regarded as entertainment. Everywhere any futile questions and curiosity are simply dismissed. Most groups are very well led; many are even remarkable in this respect, showing knowledge of the true principles of science. All participants are united in intent with the Parisian Society of Spiritist Studies, and have no other flag than the principles taught by *The Spirits' Book*.[1] Perfect order and retreat generally reigns in the proceedings; I have seen some meetings in Lyon and Bordeaux, usually composed of one hundred to two hundred persons, whose attire would not be more adequate for attending a church service. It was in Lyon that the most important general meeting was held, it was composed of more than six hundred delegates from different groups, and everything went perfectly.

Let me add that nowhere have the meetings been met with the slightest opposition, and I must be thankful to the civil authorities for showing signs of goodwill toward me at many occasions.

Mediums are also multiplying, and there are few groups that do not have many of them, not to mention the much larger number of those who do not belong to any mediumistic meeting, and use their faculty only for themselves, their families and friends. In number, there is a great majority of writing mediums of different styles, with a predominance of moralistic mediums, not pleasing for the curious, who would do better to seek amusements elsewhere and not in serious Spiritist meetings. Lyon has several remarkable drawing mediums, a medium oil painter who has never learned either drawing or painting, and several seeing mediums whose faculty I could verify myself. In Marennes, there is also a lady, a drawing medium, who

---

1 [Trans. note] A. KARDEC, *The Spirits' Book* (2nd. ed. New York: USSC/USSF, 2016).

is also a very good writing medium for dissertations and evocations. At Saint-Jean d'Angély, we saw a motor medium[2] that can be considered exceptional; it is a lady who writes long and beautiful communications while reading her newspaper or making conversation, and without looking at her hand. She sometimes even fails to notice when she has finished. Illiterate mediums are also quite numerous, and one often sees them write without having ever learned how to write. This is no more surprising than seeing a medium draw without having learned how to draw. But another characteristic is the obvious diminution in the number of physical effects mediums, as intelligent effects mediums multiply bringing spirit communications. This is happening because, as the spirits have said, the period of mere curiosity has passed, and we are now in the second period, which is that of philosophy. The third period, which will begin shortly, will be its application in reforming humanity.

The spirits, which conduct things very wisely, first wished to draw attention to this new order of phenomena, and to prove the manifestation of beings of the invisible world. By piquing their curiosity, they addressed themselves to everyone, whereas an abstract philosophy presented from the start would have been understood only by a small number of people, and it would have been difficult to admit its origin. By gradual advances,

---

2 [Trans. note] A medium specialized in automatic writing.

they showed what they could do; yet since ultimately the moral consequences were the essential goal, they took a serious tone when they deemed the number of people willing to listen to them to be sufficient, while caring little for the recalcitrant. Now, when Spiritist science has been solidly constituted, when it has been completed and rid from all the erroneous, systematic ideas which are debunked daily after careful examination, it will take care of its universal establishment by powerful means. In the meantime, they have sown the idea among everyone, so that when time is ripe, it will find landmarks everywhere, and they will then be able to overcome any obstacles, for what can human obstacles avail against the will of God?

This rational and prudent course of action is shown in everything, even in the teaching of details, which they grade and adjust according to the times, places and human habits. A bright and sudden light does not enlighten, it dazzles; so the spirits only introduced it little by little. Whoever follows the progress of Spiritist science recognizes that it grows in importance as it penetrates deeper mysteries. Today, it is tackling ideas that one could not even suspect a few years ago, and it did not say its last word on the subject because it has many other revelations.

I have acknowledged this gradual march of education from the nature of the communications obtained in the different groups I have visited, compared with those of the past. They are differentiated not only by their extent, their scope, the ease of obtaining them, and their high morality, but especially by the nature of the ideas with which they deal, sometimes in a masterly manner. This probably depends a great deal on the medium, but that is not all: it is not enough to have a good mediumistic instrument. It takes a good musician to produce beautiful sounds, but this musician needs listeners who are capable of understanding and appreciating the music, otherwise he or she would not bother to play in front of the deaf.

Moreover, such progress is not general. Apart from the mediums, we have constantly seen it in relation to the character of the groups. It reaches its greatest development in those where the purest sentiments and the most absolute moral disinterestedness with the most lively faith, do reign supreme; since the spirits know very well where they can put their trust for things that cannot be understood by everyone. In groups with less lofty conditions, the teaching is still good, always moral, but rather confined to general platitudes.

By moral disinterestedness, I mean self-denial, humility, an absolute lack of false pride, or any thought of domination by means of Spiritism. It would be superfluous to speak of material disinterestedness, because it goes without saying, and moreover because we have seen everywhere an instinctive repulsion against any idea of financial gain, which would be regarded as sacrilege. Professional and not disinterested mediums cannot be found anywhere we went, with the exception of one city which had a few. Anyone who, in Bordeaux or elsewhere, would make a profession of their faculties, would inspire no confidence; moreover, such individuals would be rejected by all groups. I am just reporting a general feeling that I have noticed.

Another characteristic feature of this period is the incalculable and ever-increasing number of followers who have not witnessed anything but are nonetheless enthusiastic believers because they have read and understood Spiritism. Regarding this, for example, they know mediums only by name and by books, and yet it would be difficult to find more faith and fervor. One of them asked me whether this ease of accepting tenets of mere theory was good or bad; if it was typical of a serious or superficial mind. I replied that the ease of accepting the idea is a sure sign of the ease of understanding it; that it can be innate as any other idea, and that a single spark then suffices to bring it out of its latent state. Such ease of understanding denotes an earlier development in this direction; it would be irresponsible to accept it blindly only on its word; yet this is not so with those who adopt it only after having studied and understood: they see through the eyes of intelligence what others see only through the eyes of the body. This proves that they attach more importance to substance than to form; for them, philosophy is foremost; the very fact of the manifestations is merely incidental. This philosophy explains to them what no other could formerly explain; it satisfies their reason by its logic, fills the emptiness of doubt in them, and that is enough for them. That is why they prefer it to anything else.

It is rare that those in this category are not good and true Spiritists, because in them lies the seed of faith, momentarily stifled by earthly prejudices. Moreover, the reasons for one's belief vary from one individual to another. To some, material proof is needed; to others, moral proofs suffice. There are still some who are not convinced by one or the other; these nuances are a diagnosis of the nature of their souls. In any case, it is difficult to count on those who say, "I will believe only if they produce the following thing," and not at all on those who believe it is beneath them to bother to study and observe. As for those who say "Even if I see it, I will not believe it, because I know it is impossible," it is useless to talk about it, and even more useless to waste time with them.

Believing is undoubtedly of great value, but belief alone is insufficient if it does not yield results, and there are unfortunately many in this situation, that is to say, for whom Spiritism is only a fact, a beautiful theory, a dead letter which does not bring about any change in their character or their habits. However, besides those Spiritists who are simply believers or sympathetic to the idea, there are Spiritists of heart; and I am happy to have met many. I have seen transformations that can be said to be miraculous; I have collected admirable examples of zeal, self-denial, and devotion, and many traits of truly Christian charity, which might rightly be called the beautiful features of Spiritism. Therefore, meetings composed exclusively of true and sincere Spiritists, those in whom the heart speaks, have a very special characteristic; all physiognomies reflect frankness and cordiality; you feel comfortable in such friendly environments, veritable temples of loving fellowship. Spirits like it as much as human beings, and it is there that they are the most expansive, that they share their innermost advices. Conversely, in those where there is divergence in feelings, where intentions are not all pure, where we may see a sardonic and disdainful smile on certain lips, where we feel the breath of ill will and pride, where at every moment one fears to step on the foot of wounded vanity, there is always discomfort, constraint and distrust. There, the spirits themselves are more reticent, and the mediums are often paralyzed by the influence of bad fluids which weigh on them like a mantle of ice. I had the pleasure of attending many meetings in the first kind, and I happily registered these seances in my notebook as among the most pleasant memories left by my trip. Meetings of this nature will certainly multiply as the true purpose of Spiritism is better understood; they are also those which make the most solid and the most fruitful dissemination, because they are addressed to serious persons, and they prepare the moral reform of humanity by preaching by example.

It is remarkable that children brought up amidst such ideas have precocious reasoning powers which make them infinitely easier to govern. I have seen many of them, of all ages and sexes, in various Spiritist families that received me at their homes, where I could see it for myself. This does not rob them of their gaiety and playfulness, but there is not in them any of that turbulence, stubbornness and caprices which render so many other children quite intolerable. On the contrary, they have an underlying sweetness, gentleness, and filial respect which makes them obedient without resistance and more diligent in their studies. This is what I have noticed, and this impression has been generally confirmed. If one would analyze here the sentiments that these beliefs tend to arouse in them, one could easily infer the effect they must produce. Let me only say that the conviction that they have of the presence of their deceased grandparents who are there, beside them, and can unceasingly see them, impresses them much more strongly than the fear of the devil, in which they would soon cease to believe; whereas they cannot doubt what they witness every single day in the bosom of their family. Therefore an ever-growing generation of Spiritists is emerging. And since these children will in turn bring up their own children in these principles, while old prejudices vanish with the old generations, it is obvious that the Spiritist idea will one day become a universal belief.

No less characteristic of the current state of Spiritism

is the development of the courage to express an opinion. If there are still followers restrained by fear, today their number has become very small in comparison to those who openly and loudly confess their beliefs and do not fear to say they are Spiritists just as any Catholic, Jew or Protestant. The weapon of ridicule has finally gone blunt by hitting without wounding; and, when facing so many notable people who have spoused the new philosophy, had to be lowered. One weapon still persists: it is the idea of the devil; but it is ridicule itself that has done it justice. Moreover, it is not only this kind of courage that I have noticed, but also that of action, dedication and self-sacrifice, that is to say, of those who in certain localities put themselves firmly at the head of the movement of new ideas, by putting themselves on the line and braving threats and suffering persecutions. They know that if fellow human beings hurt them in this short life, God will not forget them.

As we know, obsession is one of the great pitfalls of Spiritism. I could not disregard such a pivotal issue, which led me to collect some important observations on it, which will be the subject of a special article in the *The Spiritist Review*,[3] in which I will speak of the possessed of Morzine, whom I have also visited in High Savoy. Let me just say here that cases of obsession are very rare among those who have made a prior and careful

---

3 [Trans. note] A. KARDEC, *The Spiritist Review* – 1862 (New York: USSF, 2019), p. 450.

study of *The Mediums' Book*,[4] attuning themselves to the principles it contains, since such persons stand on their guard, watching for the slightest signs that could betray the presence of a suspicious spirit. I have seen some groups which are evidently under an abusive influence, because they indulge in it and yield by a too blind trust and certain moral dispositions. Others, in contrast, have such fear of being deceived that they become excessively suspicious, so to speak, scrutinizing each and every word, and thought, with meticulous care; preferring to reject what is doubtful than to submit themselves to the admission of anything bad. Also, deceiving spirits, seeing that they have nothing to gain from a mediumistic group, end up by going away, and make up for it by attaching themselves to those whom they know to be less difficult, where they can find some weaknesses and rifts to exploit. Everything in excess is harmful; but in such a case it is better to err through too much prudence than through too much confidence.

Another result of our trip was to allow us to assess the general opinion about some publications that differ more or less from our principles, with some of which being frankly hostile to it.

Let me say first of all that I have met with unanimous approval regarding my silence about any attacks aimed at my person, and that I still receive daily letters

---

4 [Trans. note] A. KARDEC, *The Mediums' Book* (2nd ed., Brasília: ISC/Edicei, 2010).

congratulating my stance on this subject. In many of the lectures given, I was highly applauded for my moderation. One of them, among others, contained the following passage: "The maliciousness of enemies produces an effect quite contrary to what they would expect, which is to make you grow even more in the eyes of your many disciples, and to tighten the bonds that unite them to you. By your lack of concern you show that you have the sentiment of your strength. By opposing meekness to insults, you give an example from which everyone can learn. History, which is our master, as well as our contemporaries, and even better than those, will take into account such moderation when readers find in your writings, that to every provocation of envy and jealousy, you have opposed the dignity of silence. Between them and you, let posterity be judge."

Personal attacks never troubled me. It could have been otherwise were they directed against Spiritism. I sometimes responded directly to some critics when I deemed it necessary, and also to prove that I could pick up the gauntlet should the situation require it. Indeed, I would have done it more often, if I had seen that such attacks were causing real harm to Spiritism. But when it was proved by facts that, far from harming it, they were serving its cause, I admired the wisdom of the spirits of employing its enemies even to propagate it, and, by revilement, to bring the Spiritist idea into circles in which it had never entered by praise. This fact was proven by my journey in striking manner since, from those very same circles, more than one supporter was recruited. When things go by themselves, why should you fight inconsequential attacks? When an army sees that the bullets of the enemy cannot reach it, it lets the enemy pull everything at its ease and exhaust its ammunition, to ensure a better campaign later on. In such a case, silence is often deceptive, since the adversary to whom I do not reply thinks that he/she has not hit hard enough or has not found out the vulnerable point. Then, confident that success will be easily obtained, they expose themselves and sink their ow ship. An immediate response would have put them on their guard. The best military commander is not the one who throws himself into the fray, but the one who knows how to wait and see. This has happened to some of my antagonists; on seeing the way they had entered, it was certain that they would sink deeper into it; I only had to let them do it. And so they did, soon discrediting their systems by their own exaggerations, much more than I could ever have done through my arguments.

However, speaking of so-called good-faith critics, I would ask nothing better than to be enlightened by them, and that, if they attack me, it should not be because of feelings of hostility or bias, or bad will, but rather to throw some light on the subject through discussion. Among these critics, there certainly are some sincere ones; but it should be remarked that those who have in mind only questions of principle discuss with calmness and never depart from propriety. Now, how many of those are there? What is featured in articles which most of the press, big or small, direct against Spiritism? Diatribes, facetious remarks generally lacking in wit, foolish and flat jokes, and often insults that vie with rudeness and vulgar triviality. Are these critics serious and worthy of an answer? There are those whose protruding ears are so conspicuous that it would seem useless to point it out, since it is a fact evident to everybody. Besides, a response would actually give them too much importance, therefore it is better to let them rub their hands in their narrow circle than to spotlight them through refutations without a cause, which would not convince them anyway. If moderation were not part of my principles, derived from those taught by Spiritism which prescribes forgetting and forgiving all offenses, I might even be encouraged to check the effect produced by such attacks, having noticed before that you are better vindicated by general opinion than by any words of your own.

As for serious, good-faith critics, who have proved their worldly wisdom by their urbanity and polish of manners, they always place science above personal matters. To those I have repeatedly replied, if not always directly, at least by seizing every opportunity to tackle the controversial issues in my writings, so that there is no objection left unanswered to anyone willing to take the trouble to read them. To answer each one individually would have required repeating the same arguments over and over again, and that would cater to only one recipient. Moreover, time would not allow me to focus on every single subject that cropped up, by writing a refutation or giving an individual explanation, while, most often, I have managed to set examples alongside the precepts, which is of benefit to all.

I had announced a small volume of Refutations. I have not published it yet, because it seemed to me that nothing was pressing immediately, and I was right. Before answering certain pamphlets which, according to their authors, were supposed to undermine the foundations of Spiritism, I wanted to gauge the effect they would produce. Well, my journey has convinced me of one thing, namely, that they have not sapped anything at all, that Spiritism is more alive than ever, and that today one hardly speaks of these pamphlets. I am well aware that in the class of individuals to whom such pamphlets are addressed, and whom I never address, they think they are unanswerable, and say that my silence is proof of my powerlessness to answer; from which they conclude that I have been utterly and completely defeated, struck down and indefensible. But what have these pamphlets achieved since it has caused me no harm? Have these writings reduced the number of Spiritists? No. Would any answer from me have converted these persons? No. There was therefore no urgency to refute them; on the contrary, it was advantageous to let them fire first.

When Sophocles was accused by his own sons,

who tried to have him declared incompetent, he refuted them by reading from his own play *Oedipus at Colonus*, which won him the trial. I am not able to produce a masterpiece like Oedipus, but others have been responsible for answering on my behalf: first my publisher, by putting in press the ninth edition of The Spirits' Book (the first was published in 1857), and the fourth of The Mediums' Book in less than two years; then the subscribers of my periodical The Spiritist Review by doubling in number and making it necessary to run a new reprint of the previous years, twice sold out; and the Parisian Society of Spiritist Studies, seeing its reputation increase. Also Spiritists, growing in number from year to year, and spreading in all directions, both in France and abroad, with meetings under the patronage and following the principles of the Paris Society. Lastly, Spiritism itself, running throughout the world, bringing comfort to the afflicted, reinvigorating people's courage, sowing hope where there was despair, confidence in the future instead of fear. These answers are worth much more than mere words, since it is facts that speak for themselves. But, as any fast courser, Spiritism raises under its feet the dust of pride, selfishness, envy and jealousy, reversing all incredulity, fanaticism and prejudices, and calling all humans to the law of Christ, that is, to charitable love, to fraternity. You who think that it is going too fast, can you stop it, or rather, can you go faster than it? The way to block its way would be quite simple:

do better than it; give more than it gives; make fellow humans better, happier, more believers than it makes, and we will leave it to follow you. But as long as you attack it only by words, and not by moral results, the charity it teaches cannot be replaced by greater charity coming from you: you will have to resign yourself to letting it go its way. This happens because Spiritism is not only a matter of facts more or less interesting or authentic, to amuse the curious; it is above all a matter of principles; it is strong above all by its moral consequences; it makes itself accepted, less by dazzling the eyes than by touching the heart – touch people's heart more than it does, and you will make yourself accepted. Now, nothing could be more ineffective at touching one's heart and reason than acrimony and insults.

If all my supporters were gathered around me, one might see something of a clique, but this could not be the case with thousands of new affiliations coming to me from all over the world, from people I have never met and who only know me through my writings. These are actual facts, corroborated by numbers, and which cannot be attributed to the effects of advertising or to any comradeship of journalism. So if the ideas that I profess, and of which I am only the humble instrument of publication, meet with so much sympathy, it is because they are not found to be lacking in common sense.

Although the usefulness of a refutations volume

that I had previously announced is no longer clearly demonstrated to me – the self-defeating attacks refuting themselves by the insignificance of their results – while the number of adherents never ceases to grow, I would nevertheless still be inclined to write it. But what I could observe during my journey has completely modified my plans, because many things do become useless, while new ideas are suggested. So I will try to do this task as quickly as possible in order not to delay the much more important work that remains to be done regarding the mission that I have undertaken.

In short, my journey had a twofold purpose: to give guidances where it might be necessary, and to instruct myself at the same time. I wanted to see things with my own eyes, to assess the actual state of Spiritism and the way in which it is understood; to study lo-cal causes which are favorable or unfavorable to its progress; to probe opinions; to appreciate the effects of opposition and criticism; and to know the opinion about certain books. I was particularly desirous to shake hands with fellow Spiritists, and to express to them personally my sincere and heartfelt sympathy in return for the touching demonstrations of loyalty and considerate affection received through their letters. To offer them, on behalf of the Parisian Society of Spiritist Studies and myself in particular, a special testimony of gratitude and admiration for those pioneers who, by their initiative, their selflessness and their devotion have been the first and firm supporters of this work, always moving forward without worrying about the stones thrown at them, and putting the interest of the cause before their personal interests. Their merit is all the greater because they work in more ungrateful soil, live in a more refractory environment, and expect no fortune, glory or honor in this world. However their joy is great when among the brambles they see some flowers blossoming. A day will come when we will be happy to raise a pantheon to Spiritists' devotion. While we await for this to happen, I would like to give them the merit of modesty: they make themselves known and appreciated solely through their actions.

Seen from these different viewpoints, this journey was very satisfying and above all very instructive for the observations it allowed me to collect. If there were any doubts as to the irresistibility of the march of Spiritism and the impotence of the attacks against it; of its moralizing influence and its future; what I have seen would suffice to dispel them. Still, there is certainly much more to be done, and in many places it has only yielded scattered scions, but such offspring is vigorous and already bears fruit. No doubt the swiftness with which Spiritist ideas propagate has been prodigious and unprecedented in the splendor of philosophies, but we are only at the beginning of the road, and most of it remains to be laid out. Therefore, let the certainty of achieving the goal act as an encouragement for all Spiritists to persevere in the path traced to them.

I have included here my main lecture given during major meetings in Lyon, Bordeaux, and some other cities. This is followed by special guidances given to specific groups in response to some of the questions that were put to me.

LECTURE

GIVEN AT GENERAL MEETINGS
OF SPIRITISTS
IN LYON AND BORDEAU

¶ 1

L adies and gentlemen, fellow Spiritists,
You are no longer schoolchildren in Spiritism; I
will leave aside today the practical details that allowed
me to recognize that you are sufficiently enlightened to
instead consider the issue from a broader perspective,
especially in its consequences. This side of the matter
is serious, no doubt the most serious, since it shows
the aim of Spiritist tenets and the means of attaining
them. It will be a little long perhaps, because the scope
of the subject is quite vast, and yet there would still
be much more to say to complete it; so I will ask your
indulgence for the fact that, being able to spend only
a short while with you, I am forced to say in one go
what I might have divided into several meetings.

Before turning to the main topic of the subject, I
think I should examine it from a somewhat personal
viewpoint. If, however, it were only an individual matter,
I would certainly not do it; but there are several general
matters connected to it, which may result in a guidance

which can benefit everyone. This is the reason that has determined me to seize this opportunity to explain the cause of certain antagonisms that I was surprised to encounter on my way.

In the current state of things, who can say that he or she has no enemies? To have none, it would be necessary not to be on Earth, because this is a consequence of the relative inferiority of our globe and its purpose as a world of atonement. Is it enough to do good deeds? Alas, no; do we not have Christ here to prove it? If then, Christ, who was goodness personified, was exposed to all sorts of wickedness one can imagine, is it any wonder that the same happens to those who are worth a hundred times less?

Speaking generally, the human being who does good must therefore expect to find ingratitude, to have against him or her those who, not doing so, are jealous of the esteem granted to those who do it. The former, not feeling strong enough to elevate themselves, seek to bring others down to their level, to deter, by denigration or slander, that which offends them. It is often said in the world that the ingratitude with which one is paid hardens the heart and makes one selfish. To speak so is to prove that one has an easily hardened heart, for that fear cannot stop the truly good individual. Recognition is already a reward for any good we do. To do so only for the purpose of receiving this reward is to do it out of interest. And then again, who knows if the one we benefit, and from whom we expect nothing in return, will not be led to better sentiments by our good actions? Maybe it is a way to make this person think, to soften his or her soul, to save it! This hope is a noble ambition; even if, in the end, we are disappointed, we will have done the right thing.

We must not believe, however, that a blessing that has remained sterile on Earth is always unproductive; it is often a seed that once sown germinates only in the future life of its recipient. I have often observed spirits, as ungrateful as humans, be touched as Spirits by the good that had been done to them; and this memory, by awakening in them good thoughts, has facilitated the way of goodness and repentance in them, and helped to shorten their suffering. Only Spiritism could reveal this outcome of charitable love; to Spiritism alone was given through communications from beyond the grave the means to show the charitable aspect of the following maxim, instead of the egoistic sense usually ascribed to it: A good action is never lost. But now let me get back to my main concern.

Any other personal matter apart, my first natural opponents are found among the enemies of Spiritism. Do not think I am sorry for it: on the contrary; the greater their animosity, the more it proves how important the new philosophical doctrine is in their eyes. If it were a thing of no consequence, like one of those utopias that are not viable from the start, they would not pay any attention to it, nor to me either. Do you not see other writings, far more disruptive to conventional ideas than mine, where the expressions used are never more sparing than the brazenness of the thoughts themselves, and which yet are allowed to pass without a whimper? It would be the same with the tenets I sought to spread if they had remained in the pages of a book. But what may seem more surprising still is the fact that I have earned adversaries even among the partisans of Spiritism – now this calls for an explanation.

Among those who embrace Spiritist ideas, there are, as you know, three very distinct categories:

1. Those who purely and simply believe in the phenomena of manifestations, but deduce no moral results from them.

2. Those who can see the moral implications, but who apply them to others and not to themselves.

3. Those who accept for themselves all the consequences of the Spiritist tenets, who practice it or endeavor to practice it morally. These, you know, are the *true Spiritists, Christian Spiritists*. This distinction is important because it explains many apparent anomalies; without that, it would be difficult to be aware of the behavior of certain people. Now, what does this morality preach? To love one another; to forgive your enemies; to return good for evil; to have no hatred, no rancor, no animosity, no envy, no jealousy; to be severe to yourself and indulgent to others. Such must be the feelings of a true Spiritist, of one who puts substance before form, and the spirit above matter. A

Spiritist may have enemies, but he or she is no one's enemy, because he does not wish evil on anyone; with even more reason do Spiritists seek to harm no one. As you can see, ladies and gentlemen, this is a general principle from which everyone can profit. Therefore, if I have enemies, they cannot be from the ranks of Spiritists in this category, since, even if admitting that they had legitimate reasons to complain against me – reasons which I strive to avoid – it would still not be a motive to blame me, unless for a very good reason, since I have never done any harm to them. Spiritism's motto is: *Without charity there is no salvation.*[5] All the more reason to add: *Without charity there are no true Spiritists.* I urge you to write this double maxim on your banner because it summarizes both the purpose of Spiritism and the duty it imposes.

Therefore, if one admits that no one can be a good Spiritist while harboring a feeling of hatred in one's heart, I flatter myself to have only friends among these latter, because if I have flaws they will know how to excuse them. We shall see to what immensely fertile consequences this principle leads.

Let us thus see the causes that may have excited certain animosities.

As soon as the first manifestations of spirits occurred, many people saw in them a means of financial gain, a new mine to exploit. If this idea had followed its

---

5 [Trans. note] In English, the word *charity* has long lost its original lofty meaning of *charitable love* used by A. Kardec.

course, you would have seen the spread of mediums, or so-called mediums, charging for consultations per seance, the newspapers would have been covered with their advertisements and publicity; and mediums would have turned into fortune tellers, with Spiritism ranked on the same level as divination, cartomancy, necromancy, etc. In this confusion, how could the public have discerned truth from lies? To rescue it from there would not have been easy. It was necessary to prevent Spiritism from taking this fatal path; it was necessary to nip this evil in the bud, otherwise it would have delayed it by over a century. I have endeavored to do this by showing, from the start, the serious and sublime side of this new science; by bringing it out of the purely experimental realm into one of philosophy and morality; finally by stressing that it would be profanation to exploit the souls of the dead, while we surround their ashes with respect. By acting thus and, without the charge of lauding myself, by pointing out the inevitable abuses that would result from such a state of affairs, I contributed to discredit the exploitation of Spiritism; and for that very reason led the public to regard it as something holy and serious.

I believe I have rendered some other services to the cause; but had I only done that, I would congratulate myself on that single achievement. Thank God, my efforts have been crowned with success, not only in France, but also abroad; and I can affirm that today professional mediums are a rare occurrence in Europe.

Wherever my books have penetrated and serve as a guide, Spiritism is seen from its legitimate perspective, that is to say, under an exclusively moral point of view. Everywhere the mediums, totally devoted and disinterested, and aware of the sacred status of their mission, are surrounded by due consideration and respect, regardless of their social position; and such consideration can only grow when they show such an altruistic disinterest despite the relative inferiority of their position.

Mind you, I do not pretend to say that among financially interested mediums there cannot be very honest and estimable individuals; but experience has proved to me and to others that interest is a powerful stimulant to fraud, because one wants to earn money, and if spirits do not yield the expected results – which often happens since they are not at our whims and caprices – then cunning, ever so fruitful in expedients, finds it easy to provide them. For one who will act loyally, there will always be a hundred that would exploit and harm the consideration enjoyed by Spiritism; and adversaries have not failed to exploit for the benefit of their criticism the frauds they witnessed, concluding that everything else must be necessarily false, and that there was reason to oppose this new-fangled quackery. In vain do we object that the holy philosophical doctrine is not responsible for these abuses; you know the adage: "When one wants to kill one's dog, one says it has rabies."

What more compelling answer can be given to the charge of quackery than to inquire: *"Who has asked you to come? How much did you pay to enter?"* The one who pays wants to be served; he/she wants to get something for their money; if they are not given what they expect, they are entitled to complain. Now, to avoid that, one will want to serve them at all costs. This is the abuse; but to prevent this threatening abuse from becoming a rule instead of being an exception, it was necessary to stop it. Now that an opinion is clearly expressed in this respect, the risk is to be feared only regarding inexperienced people. To those who would therefore complain of having been duped, or of not having obtained the answers they desired, we may say: If you had studied Spiritism, you would have known under what conditions you can fruitfully observe it; what are the legitimate grounds for confidence or distrust; what can be expected from it; and you would not have asked from it what it cannot give. You would not have consulted a medium as a fortune-teller, to ask from the Spirits revelations, information about inheritances, discoveries of hidden treasures, and a hundred other similar things which are of no concern to Spiritism. If you have been misled, you should only blame yourself.

It is quite obvious that the contribution paid by a Spiritist society to meet the expenses of the meetings cannot be considered as an exploitation. The most basic sense of fairness would grant that these fees cannot be imposed on the receiver, if he/she is neither rich enough nor able to free enough of their time to devote full attention to them. Speculation consists in making an industry of the thing, to solicit money from indifferent laypersons who have come only out of curiosity. A society that would do so would be just as reprehensible, even more reprehensible than an individual, and would no longer deserve to be trusted. That a society should provide for all its needs; that it should meet all its expenses, and not allow them to fall on one person alone, is no more than fairness, and does not constitute exploitation or speculation. However that would be different if the newcomer could buy the right to enter a meeting by paying a fee, because it would be a distortion of the essentially moral and instructive purpose of meetings of this kind, turning them into a sort of curiosity show. As for the mediums, they have multiplied in such numbers that professional, paid mediums have become completely superfluous today.

Such, ladies and gentlemen, are the ideas which I have endeavored to make prevail, and I am happy to have succeeded more easily than I would have expected; but you understand that those whose hopes I have foiled are not my friends. So this is already a category of individuals who cannot see me with good eyes, a fact worries me very little. If ever the exploitation of Spiritism tries to break into your city, I invite you to reject this new industry, so as clear yourselves from any solidarity with it, and the complaints to which it could give rise would not fall back on the pure tenets of Spiritism.

Besides material speculation, there is what might be called moral speculation, that is to say, the satisfaction of one's pride, of narcissistic self-love; those who, without pecuniary interest, thought they could make of Spiritism an honorary footstep to put themselves in evidence. I do not regard them in a more favorable light, and my writings, as well as my advices, have thwarted more than one premeditation, showing that the qualities of a true Spiritist are self-abnegation and humility according to this saying of Christ: "Whoever exalts himself will be humbled, and whoever humbles himself will be exalted."[6] Therefore, this is a second category of individuals who do not wish me any good, and which could be called the one of frustrated ambitions and crushed narcissism.

Then there are those people who do not forgive me for having succeeded; for whom the success of my books is a source of great chagrin; and to whom the testimonials of sympathy addressed to me prevent sleep. This is the clique of jealous individuals, which is not more benevolent than the other categories – far from it – and which comes reinforced by people who by temperament cannot see anyone raise their head just a little, without promptly firing at them.

---

6 [Trans. note] Matthew 23:12 ESV.

An even more irascible group of individuals, believe it or not, is found among the mediums – not paid, interested mediums but those who are quite disinterested, materially speaking, I am referring to obsessed mediums, or rather, fascinated ones. Some observations on this issue will not come amiss.

By pride they are so convinced that what they obtain is sublime, and can only come from Higher Spirits, that they are irritated by the slightest criticism, to the point of quarreling with their friends when they have the awkwardness of not admiring what is plainly absurd. This is the proof of bad influences that dominate them because, even if one assumes that, due to a lack of judgment or instruction, they cannot see clearly, this would not be a motive to take a dislike to those who do not share their opinion. However that would not suit the obsessing spirits, which, to better keep the mediums under their control, inspire them with estrangement, even aversion for anyone who could open their eyes.

Then there are those whose susceptibility is pushed to extremes; who crumple about the least thing: the place they are given to sit in a meeting and which do not put them in enough prominence; the order assigned to the reading of their communications; or when the reading excludes those whose subject does not seem opportune for an assembly; or that we do not solicit them for advice with sufficient reverence. Others find fault that the order of proceedings will not be changed to suit their personal preferences; others still would like to pose as the mediums of this or that group or society, to call the shots in the meetings, and claim that their spirit guides should be taken as absolute arbiters in all matters, etc. Such motives are so childish and so petty that one does not dare to confess them; but they are nonetheless the source of a dull animosity which betrays itself sooner or later, either by bad will or by distancing from the group. Having no good reasons to give, there are some who do not scruple to allege pretexts or fictitious reasons. Being unwilling to bow to all these pretensions, it is wrong – what am I saying! – an unforgivable crime in the eyes of some people that I have thus incensed, which is perhaps even wronger of me to worry about them or the others. Unforgivable! Do you conceive this word from people who call themselves Spiritists? This word should be removed from Spiritism's vocabulary.

This discomfort has also been felt by most group or society directors, therefore I entreat them to follow my example, that is to say, not to rely on mediums that are more of a hindrance than a relief; with them one is always uncomfortable, fearing to ruffle them by the slightest word or action.

Such inconvenience was more frequent earlier than it is now; when mediums would be scarcer, and you had to content yourself with those who were on hand. Yet today, as they visibly proliferate, the inconvenience has diminished by the very fact of the possibility of choice, while at the same time there has been an improved understanding of the true principles of Spiritism.

Apart from the degree of their mediumistic faculties, the essential qualities of a good medium should be humility, simplicity and dedication. He/she must give their assistance in order to render themselves useful, and not to satisfy their vanity. They must never take sides concerning the communications he/she receives, otherwise he/she would make others doubt their neutrality, and think that they have some interest in defending a case. Furthermore, they should accept criticism from others, even solicit it, and submit to the opinion of the majority without any ulterior motive, whether what he or she writes is false, bad or detestable; which one must be able to tell them without fear of hurting them, because after all a medium has nothing to do with it. These are the mediums who are really useful in a meeting and from whom one will never experience any inconvenience, because they understand Spiritism, whereas others do not understand it or do not want to understand it at all. The former are also those who end up obtaining the best communications because they do not let themselves be dominated by proud spirits. Deceiving spirits actually dread them because they know they cannot mislead or exploit them.

And then comes the category of people who are never satisfied: some find that I am going too fast, others that I am going too slowly; it is really like the fable of *The Miller, his Son and the Donkey*.[7] The first reproach me for having formulated premature principles in order to pose as head of a philosophical school. Aside from any Spiritist idea, would I have no right to create, like so many others do, a philosophy of my own, even if it were absurd? If my principles are false, what else would they put in their place, and would they prevail? It seems that in general one does not find my principles too unreasonable, since they have conquered so many adherents – but would that not be the very reason why they stir up a bad mood in certain people? If those principles found no partisans, if they were ridiculous to begin with, no one would be talking about them.

As for those who claim that I am not going fast enough, and would like to push me supposedly with good intention, I am willing to believe it, for it is better to believe good than evil, in which I do not wish to

---

7 [Trans. note] LA FONTAINE, *The Miller, his Son and the Donkey*: "A miller and his young son carry their donkey through the village. As several villagers mock them, the miller sets the donkey on its feet and has his son ride it. Other villagers mock them for allowing the boy instead of the old man to ride the donkey. When the miller rides the donkey, they are again mocked. Why is the son not also riding the donkey instead of following along behind? Both ride the donkey, only to be mocked again for tiring the poor animal. The miller shrugs his shoulders and decides that since it is impossible to content everyone, in the future he will transport the donkey as he pleases." Excerpted from A. LUST, *Bringing the Body to the Stage and Screen* (Lanham: The Scarecrow Press, Inc., 2012), p. 163.

engage myself. Without letting myself be influenced by the ideas of others, I follow my course; I have a goal, I see it, I know when and how I will reach it, and do not worry about the clamor of passers-by.

As you can see, Ladies and Gentlemen, my path is full of stones; as I move on they get bigger and bigger. If we knew the true cause of certain antipathies and estrangements, we would be very much surprised at many things. Besides the people who have put themselves in false, ridiculous or compromising situations in order to attack me – and who use underhanded tactics to justify themselves by resorting to small calumnies – there are also those who had hoped to draw me to them through flattery, thinking they would steer me to their designs, but who have recognized the uselessness of their maneuvers to convert me to their views. Then there are those whom I have neither flattered nor praised as they wanted me to do. And, finally, those who do not forgive me for having exposed them, and who are like a serpent on which one steps. If only for a moment all these people would rise above earthly concerns, and see things from a little higher up, they would realize how extremely puerile their worries are, and would not be surprised at the lack of importance attached to them by every true Spiritist. It is because Spiritism opens up horizons so vast that bodily life, being so short and ephemeral, vanishes together with all its vanities and small intrigues before the infinity of spiritual life.

I must not, however, fail to mention a reproach which was addressed to me: it is that I have done nothing to bring back to me the people who distanced themselves. This is true, and if it is a well-founded reproach, I deserve it, for indeed I have never taken a step for the sake of it, and here are the reasons for my indifference.

Those who come to me, it is because it suits them to do so, more on account of their sympathy for the principles I profess than because of me personally. Those who go away do so because I do not agree with them, or our ways of seeing things do not coincide – so why would I annoy them by trying to impose myself on them? It seems more appropriate to leave them alone. I really would not have the time, for we all know that my occupations do not leave me a moment's rest, and for one person that goes away, there are a thousand coming in. I owe it to the latter to put them first and foremost, and that is what I do. Is it pride? Is it scorning? Certainly not. I do not despise anyone; I pity those who do wrong, I pray to God and the good spirits to bring them back to better feelings, and that is it. If they come back, they are always welcome, but to run after them, this I never do, because of the time that people of good will demand from me, and also, because I do not attach to certain people the importance they attach to themselves. For me, a person is a person, and nothing more; I measure one's value by one's actions and feelings, and not by his or her rank. Even if they are highly placed in society, if they behave badly, if they are selfish and vain of their position, in my eyes they fall beneath a humble workman who acts well, and I would more cordially shake hands with a humble person whose heart speaks, than that of an eminent person whose heart says nothing; the first warms me, the second leaves me cold.

Although people of the highest rank honor me with their visit, never has a proletarian been kept waiting because of them. Often in my living room a prince will sit side by side with a working-class individual; if the latter were demeaned, I would promptly say that the former is not worthy to be a Spiritist; but I can happily attest that I have often seen them shaking hands, and then I said to myself: "Spiritism, here is one of your miracles; a forerunner of many wonders to come!"[8]

It was up to me to open the doors of the world at large; I had never knocked on them; it would take me a while, which I think I could use more usefully elsewhere. First and foremost there are consolations to give to those who suffer; to restore courage to those who are giving way; to rescue the other person from bad passions or despair and suicide; maybe to stop one from going downhill on the path of crime – is it not better than to be on the heights of gilded fame? I keep thousands of letters which for me are worth more than all the honors of Earth, and which I regard as my

---

8 [Trans. note] In 1862, class division and prejudice still prevailed in France, despite the French Revolution of 1789.

true titles of nobility. So do not be surprised if I let go of those who do not seek me out.

I have opponents, I know it; but their number is not so great as one might think from the enumeration above. They belong in the categories I have mentioned, but they are still only individuals, and their number is small compared to those who wish to show sympathy. Besides, they have never succeeded in disturbing my peace of mind; never have their machinations or invectives moved me in the least; and I must add that this profound indifference on my part, the silence I have opposed to their attacks, has contributed somewhat to their exasperation. No matter what they do, they will never succeed in making me abandon my restraint, which is my rule of thumb. They will never be able to say that I have responded to insult with insult. People who know me intimately can attest that I never care about such individuals; nor have I ever said a single word or made a single allusion to them at the Parisian Society of Spiritist Studies. Furthermore, in the pages of *The Spiritist Review*, I never responded to their attacks, when they were addressed directly to me; and God only knows if these were missed opportunities.

What can their bad intentions be? Nothing, neither against Spiritism, nor against myself. The doctrine proves by its gradual progress that it fears nothing. As for me, I do not hold any position, so nothing can be taken away from me. I demand nothing, I do not ask for anything, so I cannot be denied anything; I owe nothing to anyone, therefore nothing can be claimed from me. I speak ill of no one, not even of those who speak evil of me; so how could they harm me? It is true that words can be imputed to me that I have not said, and that has been done to me more than once. Yet those who know me are aware of what I could possibly say and what I would never say – and I thank those who, in such situations, have been kind enough to answer on my behalf. What I do say, I am always ready to repeat it in presence of anyone; and when I claim not to have said or done something, I think I have a right to be believed.

Besides, what are all these things compared to the ultimate goal that we, sincere and devoted Spiritists, pursue; this immense future which unfolds before our eyes? Believe me, Ladies and Gentlemen, we should regard it as a theft made from the great cause all these instants that one steals from it to worry about these trifles. For my part, I thank God, for the relief of some passing tribulations, for having already given me so many moral compensations in this world, and the joy of witnessing the triumph of Spiritism.

Please excuse me, Ladies and Gentlemen, for having talked so much about myself, but I thought that it was useful to establish a clear position so that you would know what to do in similar circumstances, and that you would be thoroughly convinced that my course of action is firmly traced, and that nothing will make me swerve from it. For the rest, I believe that from these very observations, irrespective of person, one can draw some useful lessons.

Now let us move on to another topic, and see where Spiritism stands currently.

II

Spiritism presents an unprecedented phenomenon in the history of philosophies, in the speed of its progress. No other philosophical doctrine has offered such an example. When one thinks of the progress it is making from year to year, one can predict, without too much speculation, a time when it will become a universal belief.

Most foreign countries participate in this movement: Austria, Poland, Russia, Italy, Spain, Turkcy, etc. have many followers and several perfectly organized Spiritist societies. I have more than one hundred registered cities where meetings regularly take place. In their number, Lyon and Bordeaux rank first. Honor to these two French cities, which are impressive for their population and their enlightenment, for having planted high and firm the flag of Spiritism. Several others wish to follow in their footsteps.

I have been able to come across many travelers; all agree that every year they find some progress in general opinion, while mocking critics diminish visibly. Yet jeering is succeeded by anger; those who used to laugh, are now angry – this is auspicious, according to an old proverb, and it makes the incredulous say that there might be some truth in it.

A fact no less characteristic is that all that the opponents of Spiritism have done to hinder its progress, far from stopping it, has triggered its growth; and it can be said that everywhere progress has been due to violent attacks. Did the press advocate it? Everybody knows that far from giving it a head start, it kicked out at it for as long as it could. Well, these kicks have only led Spiritism to advance. This was also the outcome of attacks of any nature directed against it.

Thus one constant remains: without the help of any means usually employed in obtaining so-called success, and despite all hindrances, it has not ceased to grow. And it grows up every day as if to deny those who predicted its imminent demise. Is this some sort of presumption or bragging? No, it is a fact that no one can deny. Spiritism has drawn its strength from itself, which proves the power of its idea. It would be better that those who thwart it would take its side instead, and resign themselves to giving way to what they cannot stop. Because Spiritism is an idea, and when an idea works, it crosses all barriers; it is not stopped at the border like a bundle of goods. Books can be burned, but the idea is not burnt, and their very ashes, carried by the wind, will fertilize the soil where it must bear fruit.

However it is not enough to launch an idea throughout the world for it to take root – certainly not. One does not create at will neither opinions nor habits; the same applies to inventions and discoveries: even the most useful will fail if it comes before its time, if the need that it is intended to meet does not exist yet. So it is with philosophical, political, religious or social doctrines; the mind must be ripe to accept them; should they come too early, they would remain in a latent state, and, like fruits grown out of season, not prosper.

If, then, Spiritism finds so many adherents, it is because its time has come, and the minds were ripe to receive it. It is because it responds to a need, to an aspiration. You have the proof of this in the number, quite considerable today, of people who welcome it without surprise, as a natural thing, when they first learn about it; and who say that it seemed to them that things had to be so, albeit without being able to define them. One feels the moral emptiness that unbelief and materialism have created around people; we understand that these doctrines dig an abyss for society; that they destroy the strongest bonds, those of loving fellowship. And then instinctively, human beings have the horror of nothingness, as much as Nature hates emptiness, therefore we welcome with joy the proof that nothingness does not exist.

But, it will be said, are we not taught every day that nothingness does not exist? No doubt it is taught to us; but how is it that incredulity and indifference have been increasing steadily for a century? It is because the proofs given to people are no longer sufficient for them today; that such proofs are no longer connected with the needs of intelligence? Scientific and industrial development have turned humans into objective individuals who want to be aware of everything and get to know the why and the how of everything. To understand in order to believe has become a compelling need, which is why blind faith no longer has any power over us. According to some this is an evil, according to others it is good; without discussing the principle, we shall say that such is the course of nature. Collective humanity, like individuals, has its infancy and mature age; when it reaches middle age, it shakes off its swaddling clothes and wants to make use of its own strength, that is, of its intelligence. To revert it backward would be as impossible as bringing a river back to its source.

To attack the merit of blind faith, some will say, is impiety, because God wants us to accept Its word without verification. Blind faith might have its raison d'être, I would even say its necessity, at a certain period of the history of humankind, If today it no longer suffices for strengthening belief, it is because it is just in human nature that it be so. Now, who made the laws of Nature? God or Satan? If it is God, there can be no impiety to follow Its laws. If today, to understand in order to believe has become a need of intelligence, just like drinking and eating are needs of the stomach, it is because God wants humans to make use of their intelligence, otherwise It would not have given it to them

in the first place. There are people who do not feel this
need; who are content to believe without verification;
I do not blame them in any way, and far be it from me
to disturb them in their tranquility. Spiritism does not
address them; as long as they have what they need, it
has nothing to give them; it does not provide food to
those who declare that they are not hungry. Spiritism
is addressed only to those whose intellectual food is
no longer sufficient. Their number is large enough so
there is no need for it to seek others; then what are
they to complain about, since it is not going after them?
Spiritism is not going to look for anyone; it imposes
itself on nobody; it limits itself to saying: Here I am,
that's what I am; that's what I bring; may those who
think they need me come and others stay as they are; I
will not disturb their consciences; I do not hurl insults
at them; I only ask them for fair reciprocity.

Why then does materialism tend to supplant faith?
Because until now faith has not reasoned; it confines
itself to saying: Believe; while materialism reasons.
These are sophisms, I agree, but whether good or
bad, they are reasons which, in the thought of many,
outweigh those who do not give any at all. Add to
that the fact that the materialistic idea satisfies those
who indulge in material life; who could not care less
about the consequences of the future; who hope by
the materialistic idea to escape responsibility for their
actions; and in short, embrace it as it is eminently
favorable to the satisfaction of all brutal appetites and

instincts. In the uncertainty of the future, humans say to themselves: Let us always enjoy the present; what do my fellow beings do for me? Why sacrifice myself for them? They are my brothers and sisters, or so they say; but what will brothers and sisters do on my behalf if *I will never meet them again!* They, maybe tomorrow, will be as dead as myself – and then what will we be for each other? Nothing, if once dead nothing remains of us. What use would it be to impose privations on myself? What compensations would I derive from it if everything ends with myself?

So try to create a society founded on fraternity with similar ideas! Selfishness would be its natural outcome. With selfishness, like a tug of war, everyone pulls the other and the strongest wins. The weak say in their turn: Let us be selfish, since the others are so; let us think only of ourselves, since the others think only of themselves.

Such is, it must be admitted, the evil that tends to invade modern society, and this evil, like a gnawing worm, can ruin it in its foundations! Oh, how guilty they are who push it in this way; who strive to kill beliefs; who advocate the present at the expense of the future! They will have a terrible account to settle for the use they have made of their intelligence!

Yet unbelief leaves a trail of anxiety after it; humans may try to deceive themselves, but they cannot help thinking sometimes of what will happen to them; the idea of nothingness gives them the chills in spite of themselves; they would like some certainty, yet they cannot find any, so they roam, they hesitate, they doubt, and doubt kills them; they feel unhappy in the midst of material enjoyments which cannot fill the abyss of nothingness which opens before them, and where they think they will be precipitated.

It is at this moment that Spiritism appears, like an anchor of salvation, like a torch in the darkness of one's soul. It comes to pluck humans from doubt; it comes to fill the horror of the void, not by a vague hope, but by irrefutable proofs which derive from the observation of facts; it comes to revive faith, not by simply saying: Believe because I say it to you, but instead: See, touch, understand and believe. Therefore it could not have come in a more opportune moment, either to stop the evil before it was irreversible, or to satisfy the needs of those who no longer believes in speech, and who wish to reason that which they believe. Materialism had seduced humans by its false reasoning; to its sophisms it was necessary to oppose solid reasoning supported by material proofs; in this struggle, blind faith was no longer powerful enough; that is why I say that Spiritism has come in its own time.

What humans are lacking is therefore faith in the future, and the idea of it given to them cannot satisfy their taste for positive facts, for it is too vague, too abstract. The links that bind it to the present are not sufficiently defined. Spiritism, on the contrary, presents the soul as a circumscribed being, similar to the human being, less the material envelope from which it has been stripped, but still covered with a fluidic envelope, a fact which is already more comprehensible, and makes one better understand the concept of individuality. Moreover, it proves through experience, the incessant relations between the visible world and the invisible world, which are thus mutually solidary. The relations of the soul with Earth do not cease with life; the soul, in the state of disembodied spirit, constitutes one of the cogs, one of the living forces of Nature. It is no longer a *useless* being thinking and acting only on behalf of itself for all eternity. Instead, it is always and everywhere an active agent of God's will which carries out Its works. Thus, according to Spiritism, everything is connected, everything is linked in the universe; and in this great, so admirably harmonious, movement, far from being extinguished, all affections survive and strengthen as they purify themselves.

If Spiritism were only a system, it would only have the advantage of being more attractive, without offering more certainty; but it is the invisible world itself that came to reveal itself to us; to prove to us that it is, not in regions of space inaccessible even to thought, but there, right by our side; that it surrounds us and that we live in its midst, as blind among seeing people. This may disturb some ideas, I agree; yet one must willingly or unwillingly bow before a fact. It may be said that this is not the case; that it must be proved that this cannot *possibly* be, by necessarily opposing to palpable proofs even more palpable proofs. Now, what does one oppose to them? A mere negation.

Therefore Spiritism is based on facts; the facts in accordance with reasoning and a rigorous logic, which somehow gives Spiritist tenets a positivist character which is appropriate to our time. Materialism has come to erode all faith and belief, to remove all basis and reason of moral principle, and to undermine the very foundations of society by proclaiming the reign of selfishness. Serious individuals then wondered where such a state of things could lead us; they have seen the abyss, and now Spiritism comes to fill it, saying to materialism, *You will go no further, for here are facts which prove the falsity of your reasoning.* Materialism threatened to shatter society by saying, *The present is everything, because the future does not exist.* Spiritism comes to take over from it by instead saying: *The present is nothing, the future is everything, and it proves it.*

An adversary has said somewhere in a newspaper that Spiritism is full of alluring details. He could not, without intending to do so, make a greater eulogy to it, while at the same time condemning himself in a more peremptory manner. To say that a thing is appealing is to say that it pleases. This is the great secret of the propagation of Spiritism. What can one oppose to it that will supplant its attractiveness? If one does not do it, it is because one has nothing better to give. What is so appealing in Spiritism? That is easy to answer.

Spiritism is appealing because:

1.   It satisfies people's instinctive yearning toward the future.

2.   It presents the future in a manner which is admissible to reason.

3.   The certainty of a future life makes one bear with patience the miseries of current life.

4.   With the plurality of existences, such miseries have a reason which is explained; so instead of accusing Providence, one finds them to be fair and accept them without murmuring.

5.   We are happy to learn that our nearest and dearest are not lost forever, that we will see them again, and that they are often next to us.

6.   All teachings given by the good spirits tend to make people do better and behave better toward one another.

There are still many other reasons that Spiritists alone can understand. Conversely, what alluring details are offered by materialism? Nothingness. This is the consolation it gives for the miseries of life.

With such elements, the future of Spiritism cannot be doubtful, and yet, an amazing fact is that it has made its way so fast through prejudices. How, and by what means, will it achieve the transformation of humanity, is what remains to be seen.

III

When we consider the current state of society, we are tempted to look at its transformation as a miracle. Well then it is a miracle that Spiritism can and must accomplish, because it is in the designs of God, and reinforced by Its watchword: *Without charity there is no salvation*. Let society take this motto as its motto, and conform its conduct to it, instead of following the one that is in the order of the day – that is, *Charity begins at home* – and all changes. And all that needs changing is to make it be accepted.

As you know, Ladies and Gentlemen, the word *charity*[9] has a very wide meaning. There is charity in thoughts, words, and actions; it is not only in giving alms. Those who are charitable in thought, are indulgent to the faults of others; charitable in words, never saying anything that could harm their neighbor; charitable in actions, by assisting others to the extent of their capabilities. The poor person who shares his/her piece of bread with a poorer one is more charitable and has more merit in the eyes of God than the one who gives what is superfluous to him/her without deprivation of anything. Whoever harbors against his/her neighbor feelings of hatred, animosity, jealousy, resentment, lack charity. Charity is the counterpart of selfishness; one is the abnegation of personality, the other the exaltation of personality. One says: For you first, and

---

9 [Trans. note] See also p. 29, footnote 5.

for me afterwards; the other: For me first, and for you if there are any left. The first is all in this teaching of Christ: *"So whatever you wish that others would do to you, do also to them"*;[10] in a word, it applies, without exception, to all social relations. It should be agreed that if all members of a society acted on this principle, there would be fewer disappointments in life. As soon as two people are together, they engage, by that very fact, in reciprocal duties. If they want to live in peace, they are obliged to make mutual concessions. These duties increase with the number of individuals. Human groups form collective wholes that also have their respective obligations; so you have besides rapports of individual to individual, those from town to town, from province to province, from nation to nation. These relations may present two motives which are the negation of one another: selfishness versus charity, for there is also national selfishness. With selfishness, self-interest comes first, everyone looks only after himself/herself, everyone sees his/her fellow human being as an antagonist, a rival who can poach our business, who can exploit us or be exploited by us. It is one trying to pull the rug out from under the feet of his/her neighbor: the victory belongs to the most skillful; and society, sad thing to admit, often hails this victory, which makes humans be divided into two main classes: the exploiters and the exploited. The result is a perpetual antagonism

---

10 [Trans. note] Matthew 7:12 ESV.

that makes life a torment, a veritable hell. Replace selfishness with charity, and everything changes; no one will seek to harm his/her neighbor; hatred and jealousy will be extinguished for lack of fuel, and humans will live in peace, helping each other instead of tearing each other apart. Once charity replaces selfishness, all social institutions will be founded on the principle of solidarity and reciprocity; the strong will protect the weak instead of exploiting them.

That is fine, dream on – some will say – yet unfortunately it is nothing but a dream, for humans are selfish by nature, by need, and always will be. If it were so, it would be very sad, and then one would deem it necessary to ask for what purpose did Christ come to preach charity to humans, if it was worth the same as preaching to animals. However, let us examine this more closely.

Is there any progress from the savage to the civilized human being? Do not we seek every day to soften the habits of the savages? For what purpose, if they were incorrigible? Strange weirdness indeed! So you hope to correct savages, yet you think that civilized humans cannot improve? If a civilized human claimed to have reached the last limit of the progress accessible to the human race, it would suffice to compare the mores, the character, the legislation, the social institutions of today with those of the past; and yet those individuals of old also thought they had reached the summit of evolution. What would a great lord of King Louis

14th's time have answered if he had been told that there could be a better, more equitable, more humane order of things than that of his time? And that this more equitable system would bring the abolition of caste privileges, and the equality between the great and the small before the law? The audacious person who would dare to say that might have paid dearly for such temerity.

From this we can conclude that humans are eminently perfectible, and that the most advanced of today may seem to be as backward in a few centuries from now as those of the Middle Ages are in comparison with us. To deny this fact would be to deny progress, which is a law of Nature.

Although humankind has gained from a moral point of view, it must be admitted that progress has been more accomplished in the intellectual sense. Why is that so? This is still one of those problems that Spiritism was given to explain, by showing that morals and intelligence are two paths that rarely go side by side. While one individual takes a few steps in one, he/she remains behind in the other. Yet later he/she regains the ground lost, and the two forces end up balancing themselves through successive reincarnations. Humans have reached a time where science, industry and the arts have achieved an unprecedented level of development. If the enjoyments we draw from them do satisfy material life, they leave a void in the soul. We long for something better: we dream of better institutions; we want life, happiness, equality and justice for all. But how to accomplish it with the vices of society, especially with egoism? Therefore humans see the necessity of good to be happy. We understand that the reign of good alone can give us the happiness to which we aspire. We sense this reign, because instinctively we have faith in the justice of God, and a secret voice tells us that a new era is about to begin.

How will this happen? Since the reign of good is incompatible with selfishness, it is necessary to destroy selfishness; but who can destroy it? A predominance of the feeling of love, which leads humans to treat one another as brothers and sisters and not as enemies. Charity is the foundation, the cornerstone of every social edifice; without it, humans can build only on sand. Therefore the efforts and especially the examples of all good individuals tend to propagate it; that they are not discouraged if they see an upsurge in bad passions. These latter are enemies of good, and seeing its advance, they rush against it; but God has allowed that to happen, since by their own excesses, they destroy one another. The apex of an evil is always a sign that it is coming to an end.

I have just said that without charity humans can only build on sand; now an example will make it even better understood.

Some well-intentioned individuals, touched by the sufferings of some of their fellow beings, believed to have found the cure for evil in some systems of social reform. With few differences, the principle is almost the same in all, whatever the name they are given. Common life to be less expensive; community of goods so that everyone has something; participation of all in collective work; no great wealth, but also no poverty. This was very attractive to those who, having nothing, already saw the purse of the rich enter into the social fund, without calculating that the totality of the pooled wealth would create general poverty instead of a partial poverty; that the equality established today would be broken tomorrow by the mobility of the population and the difference of individual aptitudes; that the permanent equality of goods presupposes an equality of abilities and work. But that is not the question; it is not my place to examine the strength and weakness of these systems; I will make abstraction of the impossibilities of which I have just spoken, and instead propose to consider them from another viewpoint, which I have no recollection of being employed before, and which is connected to the subject at hand.

The authors, founders or promoters of all these systems, without exception, have proposed the organization of material life in a way which may be profitable to all. The goal is unquestionably laudable; It remains to be seen whether, in this building, there is no lack of the foundation which alone could consolidate it, admitting it to be practicable.

What they have in common is the most complete abnegation of self, each one having to sacrifice his/

her own personality, which requires the most absolute devotion. Now, the motive of self-denial and devotion is *charity*, that is, the love of neighbor. But we have acknowledged that the foundation of charity is belief; that the lack of belief leads to materialism, and ma terialism to egoism. In a system which, by its nature, requires for its stability moral virtues in the highest degree, it would be necessary to take its starting point in the spiritual element. Well then, not only is the latter ignored, the material side being its sole object, but many of these systems are based on a highly avowed materialist doctrine, or on pantheism, which is a kind of disguised materialism; that is to say, ornamented with the beautiful name of *fraternity*. But fraternity, as well as charity, can neither be imposed nor forced by decree; it must be in one's heart; it is not a system that will give birth to it if it is not already there, while the opposite, which is the rule, will ruin the system and make it fall into anarchy, because everyone will want to seek their own interests. Experience is there to prove that it does not stifle ambition or greed. Before doing anything for people, it would be necessary to train people for it, as one trains workers before entrusting them with a job. Before building, it is necessary to make sure of the solidity of the construction materials. Here solid materials will be individuals of heart, dedication and self-sacrifice. With selfishness, love and fraternity are but idle words, as I have said. How then, under the empire of egoism, could we find a system that requires self-denial to a degree which is all the greater, for its essential principle is the solidarity of all for each and every one, and one for all? Some of these people left their native land to establish colonies elsewhere, under a regime of fraternity. They wanted to escape the selfishness that crushed them, but instead selfishness followed them, and again there were exploiters and exploited because charity was lacking. They believed that it was enough for them to take as many arms as possible, without thinking that they were at the same time taking with them the gnawing worms of their institution, which was ruined all the more quickly since they had neither sufficient moral nor material power over them.

What they needed was fewer arms and more strong hearts. Unfortunately many followed them only because, incapable to do anything elsewhere, they thought they would be exempt from certain personal obligations; they saw only a seductive goal, without noticing the thorny path to reach it. Disappointed in their hopes when they realized that before they could enjoy life, they would have to do much work, much self-sacrifice, and undergo much suffering, they envisioned the prospect of discouragement and despair – and you know what happened to most of them. Their fault was to have wanted to erect a building starting from the top, before seating it on a solid foundation. Study the history and the reason for the fall of most prosperous nations fall, and everywhere you will find the hand of egoism, greed and excessive ambition.

Without charity, there is no stable human institution, and no charity or fraternity is possible in the true sense of the word, without belief. So apply yourself to develop those feelings which, as they grow, will kill the selfishness that kills you. The day charity penetrates the masses, when it becomes faith, the religion of the majority, then human institutions will improve themselves by force of circumstances. Abuse, born of a feeling of personality, will then disappear. Therefore teach charity, and above all, preach by example: it is the anchor of salvation of society. It alone can bring the reign of good to Earth, which is the reign of God. Without it, whatever you do, you will only create utopias from which you will derive only disappointment. If Spiritism is true, if it must regenerate the world, it is because it is based on charity. It has not come to overthrow traditional worship, nor to establish a new one; it proclaims and proves the truths that are common to all and form the basis of all religions, without worrying about details. It only destroys one thing: materialism, which is the negation of all religion; and overthrows only one temple: that of selfishness and pride, giving a practical sanction to those words of Christ which summarize his whole law: *"Love your neighbor as yourself."* Do not be surprised, therefore, that its adversaries are the worshipers of the golden calf, whose altars it breaks down. Spiritism naturally has against it all those who find its moral principles troublesome, those who would willingly made a pact with spirits and their manifestations, if the spirits had contented themselves with amusing them; if they had not come to dismiss their pride, to preach self-denial, disinterestedness, and humility. Let them say and do what they want; things will still follow the course which is in the designs of God.

Therefore Spiritism, through its powerful revelation, hastens social reform. Its adversaries will no doubt laugh at this claim, and yet it is not presumptuous. I have shown that unbelief, the mere doubt about the future, leads humans to focus on current life, which quite naturally develops a feeling of selfishness. The only remedy for evil is to focus one's attention on another point and to disorient it, so to speak, in order to make it lose its habits. Spiritism, by patently demonstrating the existence of the invisible world, inevitably brings a very different order of ideas, for it enlarges the moral horizon confined to Earth. The importance of bodily life diminishes as the importance of spiritual life grows; quite naturally we place ourselves at another viewpoint, and what seemed to be a mountain now seems but a grain of sand. All the vanities, the ambitions of this world become puerile, childish rattles in presence of the grand future that awaits us. By ascribing less value to earthly things, one seeks less to satisfy oneself at the expense of others; hence a decrease in the feeling of selfishness.

Spiritism does not limit itself to proving the existence of an invisible world. By the examples which it unfolds before our eyes, it shows the latter in its reality, and not as the imagination would have conceived it; it shows it peopled with happy or unhappy beings, yet it proves that charity, the sovereign law of Christ, can alone guarantee happiness. Conversely, we see earthly society tearing itself apart under the rule of selfishness, whereas it could live happily and peacefully under the rule of charity.

Therefore everything is beneficial for human beings with charity: happiness in this world and happiness in the world beyond. It is no longer, to use an expression coined by a materialist, the sacrifice of fools. Rather, like that used by Christ, it is profit returned to us a hundredfold. With Spiritism, humans understand that they have everything to gain by doing good, and everything to lose by doing evil. But, between, I will not say luck, but the certainty of losing or winning, the choice itself cannot be doubtful. So the propagation of the Spiritist idea necessarily tends to make individuals better for one another. What it does today to individuals, it will do to the masses when it becomes generally known. Let us try to spread it in the interest of each and every one.

I foresee an objection that could be raised if one

said that, according to these ideas, the practice of good would be an interested calculation. To this I answer that the Church, by promising the joys of heaven or by threatening with the flames of hell, itself leads people by hope and fear; that Christ himself said that what we freely give in this world would revert a hundredfold. Doubtless, there is more merit to do good spontaneously without thinking of consequences, but not all persons have reached this point; and it is better to do good with an ulterior motive than no good at all.

It is sometimes said of people who do good without any premeditated design and without even suspecting it, so to speak, have no merit, because they spent no efforts in making it. Well, this is a mistake. Human beings achieve nothing without effort; he or she that apparently has nothing left to do in the current existence must have struggled in a previous one, and goodness has ended up identifying itself with them, which is why it seems quite natural to them. There are good things in such people, as in others, ideas which also have their source in an earlier work. This is another problem that Spiritism is solving. So good individuals have also had the merit of struggle. For them the victory is won, while others have yet to conquer it; that is why, as with children, you need a stimulus, that is, a goal to achieve or, if you want, a prize to win.

There is an even more serious objection. If Spiritism produces all these results, then Spiritists must be the first to benefit from them. Abnegation, selfless devotion, indulgence for others, absolute abstention from any speech or action that could harm fellow beings; in a word, charity in its purest sense; must be the invariable rule driving them. They must know neither pride nor jealousy, nor envy, nor rancor, nor silly vanities, nor the puerile susceptibilities of self-love. They must do good for good's sake, unassumingly and without ostentation. By practicing this maxim of Jesus Christ, *"Do not let your left hand know what your right hand is doing,"* no one will deserve to be included in this verse of Racine:

"Fault-finding with someone's good action is always a disguised offense."

In short, the most perfect harmony must reign among Spiritists. Why, then, are there examples which seem to contradict the efficacy of these fine maxims?

In the beginning, spirit manifestations were accepted by many who did not foresee their consequences. Most saw in them only more or less curious effects. However when a strict moral code came out of them, with rigorous duties to fulfill, many did not feel the strength to put it into practice and conform themselves to it. They have not had the courage of devotion, self-denial, or humility; in them the physical nature has prevailed over the spiritual nature. They were able to believe, but shrank from its fulfillment. Therefore in the beginning there were only Spiritists, that is to say, believers. However philosophy and morals have opened up to this science a new horizon, and created *Practicing Spiritists*. Some lagged behind, others moved forward.

As morals became more sublime, the more they brought out the imperfections of those who did not wish to follow those standards, as a bright light enhances shadows. It was like a mirror: some did not want to look in it or, thinking they recognized themselves in it, preferred to throw a stone at its reflection. This is still the cause of certain animosities; but I am happy to say that these are exceptions; like a few black spots in a huge painting, that cannot alter its overall brightness. They belong largely to what might be called first generation Spiritists, whereas the great majority of those who have been formed since and are formed every day have accepted its tenets precisely because of its morals and philosophy, which they strive to practice. To pretend that they must all have become perfect would be to misunderstand the nature of humanity; but if they have stripped off only a few parts of the old human being, this will always be a progress which must be taken into account. Inexcusable in the sight of God are only those who, being well and duly enlightened, would not profit as best they could from it. These, of course, will have a serious account to settle, whose consequences, as shown by many examples, they will experience even while here on Earth. However, beside these, there are many individuals who have undergone a real metamorphosis and found in the Spiritist belief the strength to overcome deeply ingrained and long-standing inclinations, to break with old habits, to let go of resentments and enmities, to shrink social distances. Miracles are asked of Spiritism: these are the ones it produces.

Thus, by the force of things, Spiritism will inevitably lead to moral improvement. Such an improvement will lead to the practice of charity, and charity will give rise to the feeling of fraternity. When humans are imbued with these ideas, they will conform to their institutions, and in this way be led naturally and without upheaval to all the desirable reforms. It is the foundation on which they will build the future social edifice.

This transformation is inevitable, because it is according to the law of progress; but if it would follow only the natural course of things, its accomplishment might take too long. If we believe in the revelation brought by spirits, it would be in God's designs to activate it, and we are living in the predicted time when this should take place. The concordance of spirit communications regarding this subject is a fact worthy to be remarked. In every quarter one hears of the arrival of a new age, and that great things will be accomplished. It would be wrong, however, to believe that the world is bound to suffer a material cataclysm. In scrutinizing the words of Christ, it is evident that in this circumstance, as in many others, he was speaking in an allegorical manner. The renewal of humanity, the reign of good succeeding the reign of evil, are rather great things that can be achieved without the need to encompass the world in some universal shipwreck; or to produce quite extraordinary phenomena; or to derogate from natural laws. It is always within this logic that the spirits have expressed themselves.

With Earth having arrived at the appointed time to become a happy abode, and thus raise its rank in the hierarchy of worlds, it suffices for God not to allow imperfect spirits to reincarnate here; to remove from Earth those who, by pride, unbelief, and bad instincts would, in a word, be an obstacle to progress and disturb good harmony, same as you would do yourself in an assembly where you wish to have peace and quiet, and from which you discard those who might bring disorder into it; or as one expels from a country the criminals whom one banishes to distant lands. So that in the species, or better saying – to use the words of Christ – out of the generation of spirits sent for atonement on Earth, those who have remained incorrigible vanish away and be replaced by a generation of more advanced spirits, a new generation of humans should suffice, together with the will of God, which can also, by unexpected but quite natural means, speed up their departure from here. If then, as it is said, most of the children born today belong to the new generation of Better Spirits, and the others go away every day to never come back, then it is obvious, that in a given time, a complete renewal will have taken place. What will become of the exiled spirits? They will go into lower-order worlds to atone for their hardening through long centuries of terrible trials, for they too are, so to speak, rebellious angels, since they have misunderstood the power of God, and rebelled against Its laws of which Christ had come to remind them.[11]

Be that as it may, in Nature nothing is rushed; the old yeast always leave its traces for some time, which then fade away little by little. When the spirits tell us – and they say it everywhere – that this moment is now arriving, do not think that we are going to witness a visible change; they are referring to a moment of transition. We witness the departure of our elders, and the arrival of new fellow beings who come to establish the new order of things, that is to say, the reign of justice and charity which is the true reign of God as predicted by the prophets and for which Spiritism comes to prepare the way.

You see, Ladies and Gentlemen, we are already far from the table turning formerly used in seances, yet only a few years separate us from the cradle of Spiritism! Whoever would have been daring enough then to predict what it would become today, would have deemed a fool in the very eyes of early adherents. While seeing a tiny seed, who could have understood, if he/she had not seen it yet, the huge tree that would come out of it? Seeing a child born in a stable in a poor village of Judea, who could have believed that without

---

11 See the article "Essay about the Interpretation of the Doctrine of the Fallen Angels" in The Spiritist Review – 1862 (January, p. 3).

pomp and circumstance, and devoid of mundane power, Jesus' mere voice would stir the world, assisted only by some ignorant and poor fishermen? Well, the same has happened with Spiritism, which, emerging from a humble and ordinary phenomenon, is already spreading its roots everywhere, with branches that will soon be sheltering the whole world? It is just that things happen swiftly when God so wishes; and who would not see the finger of God in it, since nothing happens without Its permission!

Witnessing the irresistible march of things, you can also say, as formerly the Crusaders did when marching to conquer the Holy Land, *It is the will of God!* But with a difference: they marched bearing iron and fire, whereas your only weapon is charity, which, instead of mortal wounds, pours a salutary balm over sore hearts. And with this peaceful weapon, which gleams in the eyes like a divine ray, and not like a deadly sword. Sowing hope and not fear, you have in a few years brought back to the fold of faith more lost sheep than several centuries of violence and constraint would have achieved. By using charity as a guide, Spiritism is conquering the world.

But is this a chimera, a wishful dream of which I have painted the picture? Certainly not, since reason, logic, experience, in short, everything shows it as a reality.

Spiritists! You are the first pioneers of this great work; make yourselves worthy of this glorious mission, of which first initiates will reap the fruit. Preach by words, but above all, preach by example, so that, when seeing you, no one can say that the precepts you teach are empty words in your mouth. Following the example of the Apostles, perform miracles – God has given you the gift – not miracles for striking the senses, but those of charity and love. Be kind to your brothers and sisters; be kind to everyone; be kind to your enemies! Following the example of the Apostles, cast out demons – you have the power and they swarm around you. These are the demons of pride, of ambition, of envy, of jealousy, of greed, of sensuality, bearers of all bad passions and bringers of discord. Drive them out of your own hearts so that you have the power to drive them out of the hearts of others. Do these miracles, and God will bless you, and future generations will bless you, as those of today bless the early Christians, many of whom are living again among you to assist and contribute in the crowning of Christ's work. Do these miracles, and your names will be inscribed with glory in the annals of Spiritism; do not tarnish it with sentiments and actions unworthy of true Spiritists, of Christian Spiritists. Expel as quickly as possible what might still remain in yourselves of the old yeast; remember that from one moment to the next, perhaps tomorrow, the angel of death may come knocking at your door and say to you: God summons you to tell what you did with Its word, the word of Its Son, Jesus, that It made the good spirits repeat to you. Be always ready to depart, and do not act like the reckless traveler who is caught off guard. Make your provisions in advance, that is to say, provisions of good works and good sentiments, for woe to those whom the fatal moment would surprise with their hearts full of hatred, envy or jealousy in the hearts. Those would be escorted by evil spirits that would rejoice at the misfortunes that await for them. These misfortunes would be their work; and you, Spiritists, know what such misfortunes are. Those who endure them come to describe their sufferings themselves. Conversely, to those who have led a true and pure life, the good spirits will say, *Fellow beings, welcome to the heavenly stay where songs of joy await you!*

Your adversaries may laugh at your beliefs in spirits and their manifestations, but they will not laugh at the qualities these beliefs offer; they will not laugh when they see enemies forgiving instead of hating one another, peace being restored between divided loved ones, former unbelievers start praying, a violent and angry individual become gentle and peaceful, a dissolute person become virtuous and care for his/her family, the proud become humble, the selfish become charitable. And they will not laugh when they see that they no longer have to fear the vengeance of an enemy who has become a Spiritist; the rich will not laugh when they see the poor no longer envious of their fortune, and the poor blessing the rich person that has become more human and more generous, instead of being jealous of him/her. Bosses will no longer laugh at their subordinates and will stop *harassing* them, when they see the latter more scrupulous and conscientious in the performance of their duties. Rulers will finally encourage those who are under their command and their tenants, when seeing them, under the influence of the Spiritist faith, more trustworthy, more dedicated, and more sincere. Everyone will say that Spiritism is good for something, if only to safeguard their material interests – so much the worse for them if they fail to see beyond it. Also under the influence of the Spiritist faith, the soldier will become more disciplined, more human, easier to lead; he/she will have a true feeling of duty, and obey orders more for reason than for fear. This is the evidence observed by all those who are in command who happen to be imbued with these principles – and they are numerous – so they assure that there is no obstacle to the propagation of these ideas among their minions.

Here, all of you who mock and laugh, is what Spiritism produces, this utopia of the nineteenth century, admittedly to a limited extent still, but whose influence is already recognizable, and soon everyone will understand that all have everything to gain from its promulgation. And that its influence is a security guarantee for social relations, because it is the most powerful obstacle that can be opposed to bad passions and tumultuous riots, showing the bond of love and fraternity that must unite the powerful to the poor and vice versa. Make it so, by your own example, that one may soon say: Would to God that all individuals were Spiritists at heart.

Dear Spiritist brothers and sisters, I have come to show you the way, to make you see the ultimate goal. May my words, weak as they are, have at least made you understand its greatness! But others will come after me, who will also show it to you, and whose voice, more powerful than mine, will have the resounding brilliance of the trumpet to all nations. Yes, my brothers and sisters, other Spiritists, messengers of God for establishing Its kingdom on Earth, will soon arise among you, and you will recognize them by their wisdom and the authority of their language. On hearing their voice, unbelievers and impious individuals will be amazed and astounded, and will lower their heads, for they will not dare to call them mad. How I wish I could reveal to you, fellow Spiritists, all that the future has in store for us! But the time is near when all these mysteries will be revealed, to the confusion of the wicked and the exaltation of the good.

While it is still time, put on your white robe, that is, smother all discords, for discords belong to the reign of evil which will end. May you all blend yourselves into one and the same family, and call yourselves, from the bottom of your hearts and without any ulterior motives, brothers and sisters. If among you there were discordances, causes of antagonism; if groups which must all march toward a common goal were divided – I say this with regret – then, without worrying about the causes, without considering who may have wronged first, I would side without hesitation with the one that practiced the most charity, that is, where abnegation and true humility prevailed, because the one who lacks charity is always wrong, regardless of being right in some other respect, and God curses the one who says to his/her brother or sister: *Raca*.[12] Groups are collective individuals who must live in peace as individuals, if they are truly Spiritists; they form the battalions of the great phalanx. Now, what would become of a phalanx whose battalions would be divided? Those who see others with a jealous eye would prove, by this alone, that they are under an evil influence, for the spirit of good cannot generate evil. As you know, we know a tree from the fruit it bears; now, the fruit of pride, envy and jealousy is a poisoned fruit that kills the one that feeds on it.

What I said about discordances among groups, can also be said of those that might exist between individuals. In such circumstances, the opinion of impartial people is always favorable to the one who proves to be loftier and more altruistic. As no one is infallible here below, reciprocal indulgence is a consequence of the principle of charity which tells us to do unto others what you wish others to do unto you; otherwise, without indulgence, there is no charity,

---

12 [Trans. note] Symbolic allusion to Matthew 5:22 AKJV/PCE: "*Whosoever shall say to his brother, Raca* [fool], *shall be in danger of the council; but whosoever shall say, Thou fool, shall be in danger of hell fire.*"

and without charity, no true Spiritist. Moderation is one of the characteristic signs of this feeling, just as acrimony and resentment are its negation. With bitterness and a vindictive disposition we mar the best causes, whereas with moderation one adds to one's own rightness if it happens to be on one's side; and one yields to the other if one is not right. If, then, I had to form an opinion in a dispute, I would be less concerned with the cause than with the consequences. The cause, especially in arguments of words, may be the result of a first initiative which is not always under your control. Then the subsequent attitude of the two adversaries will be the result of reflection: they thus act in cold blood, and it is then that the true natural character of each one of them reveals itself. A stubborn head and a good heart often go together, but bearing a grudge is incompatible with having a good heart. My measure of appreciation would therefore be charity, that is to say, I would ascertain which one speaks less evil of his/her adversary, and is the most moderate in his/her recriminations. It is on this measure that God will judge us, for It will be indulgent to those who have themselves been indulgent; and inflexible to those who have been inflexible.

The path traced by charity is clear, infallible and unmistakable. It could be defined as A sentiment of benevolence, justice and indulgence toward the neighbor, based on what one would like the neighbor to do unto oneself. Taking it as a guide, one will be sure not to deviate from the right path, which is the one that leads to God: whoever sincerely and seriously wants to work for its improvement, must analyze charity in its most minute details, and conform one's conduct to it, for it applies to all circumstances in life, whether large or small. When uncertain about a party to take regarding others, one only has to quest for the presence of charity, and it will always answer right. Unfortunately we listen more often to the voice of selfishness.

Therefore probe the folds of your soul to tear out the last vestiges of bad passions, if there are still traces of them in your inner self; and if you bear a grudge against someone, hasten to stifle it, and say to your adversary: Brother/sister, let us forget the past; evil spirits have divided us, so let the good ones unite us! If someone refuses the hand you offer them, then pity him or her, for God will say to them: Why do you ask for forgiveness, you who have not forgiven? Hurry up, so that these fatal words are not applied to you: It is too late.

Such, my fellow Spiritists, is the advice that I have chosen to give to you. The trust which you confided to me is a guarantee that those recommendations will bear fruit. The Good Spirits who assist you tell you the same thing every day, but I thought I had to present the whole issue to better highlight the consequences. I therefore come, in their name, to remind you of the great law of love and fraternity which is to govern the world and to bring peace and concord under the banner of charity for all without any distinctions of religion, sect, caste, or race.

By raising this banner, Spiritism will be the link that will bring closer together humans divided by worldly beliefs and prejudices. It will lower the strongest barriers that separate peoples, such as national antagonism. Under the shadow of this banner, which will be their rallying point, people will get used to seeing brothers and sisters in those in whom they saw only enemies. By then there will be more struggles, because evil does not let go easily of its prey, and material interests are tenacious. The accomplishment of this work to which you have contributed, you will certainly not see with your eyes of flesh, although the moment is not so far away; and the first years of the next century should already point out to this new era, whose path is being prepared at the end of the current one, But you will enjoy through your own spirit sight the good you have done, just as the martyrs of Christianity have enjoyed seeing the fruits of their shed blood. So let us be of good courage and always persevere. Do not be angry with obstacles: a field does not become fertile without the sweat of one's labor; just as parents in their old age built a house for their children, remember that you now build a temple in the universal loving fellowship for future generations, in which the only offerings to be immolated are selfishness, pride and all the bad passions that have bloodied humanity.

SPECIFIC INSTRUCTIONS

GIVEN TO GROUPS IN
RESPONSE TO SOME OF
THEIR QUESTIONS

1

There is one issue to which I would like to draw your close attention: I am referring to the hidden maneuvers of the opponents of Spiritism, who, after having unsuccessfully attacked it openly, now try to do it covertly. Be warned, this is a tactic against which you should be on your guard.

As you know, Spiritism has been fought by every possible means. It has been attacked in the name of reason, science, religion – nothing has succeeded. It has been ridiculed high and low, yet mockery has slipped upon it like water on the marble. Threats and persecutions did not thrive either: if they found a few reeds, they have encountered massive oak trees which they have not been able to bend. Moreover, have been unable to shake anyone's conviction. Do you believe that our enemies have surrendered? Certainly not; they still have two means, a last resource which, I hope, will not serve their purpose any better, thanks to the common sense and the watchfulness of all true Spiritists. These will be able to preserve themselves from enemies within just as they have repulsed those from outside.

Having not been able to ridicule Spiritism, which proved invulnerable under the auspices of its sublime morality, they now seek to mock Spiritists, that is, to elicit ridiculous behavior on the part of *so-called* Spiritists, or make them responsible for the ridicule of others. What they would like most of all is to be able to associate the words Spiritism, Spiritist and Medium with those of charlatans, illusionists, necromancers and fortune-tellers, and it would not be difficult for them to find complacent accomplices in this deed, who would employ mystical or cabalistic signs somehow justifying what certain newspapers have dared to claim, that Spiritists engage in practices of magic and witchcraft, and that their meetings remind scenes of a witches' sabbath. At the sight of a mountebank's poster announcing performances of American or other mediums, such as the Northern Hercules, they rub their hands in glee and shout from the roofs that serious Spiritism is nothing but a vulgar circus act to watch from the bleachers.

True Spiritists would never give them the satisfaction; and reasonable, rational people will always tell the difference between seriousness and parody. Nevertheless they must be on their guard against any incitement that might give rise to some criticism; in this case, it is necessary to avoid even appearances. A capital point to give a formal denial to such allegations of ill intent, is one's disinterestedness. What about those people who do everything for nothing and only for commitment to others? How to call them charlatans if they ask for nothing in return? Who would dare say that they live from Spiritism just as others live from their professional earnings? Those who have no interest whatsoever in fraud, and for whom, on the contrary, their belief offers an occasion for self-sacrifice and self-denial? Who seek neither honors nor profits? I repeat, moral and material disinterestedness will always be the most irrefutable answer to detractors of Spiritism; that is why they would be delighted to find any pretext to take away this prestige, even if they had to pay people to play a farce – for us to behave otherwise would provide them with ammunition. Do you want proof? Here is what can be read in an article published by the *Courrier de l'Est*, a Bar-le-Duc's newspaper, which was reproduced by the *Courrier du Lot*, of Cahors, among other periodicals whose sole purpose is to find something to sting:

"... Spiritism counts as its partisans three different classes of individuals: those who *live from it*, those who are amused by it, and those who believe in it. Magistrates, doctors, serious people also give in to this practice, innocent for them, but much less so for the class of individuals who *live from it*. Mediums today form *a category of unlicensed professionals who yet make a trade, a real business that I will now explain ...*"

After that, there is a long article seasoned by not very witty jibes, describing a seance attended by the article's author, with the following passage referring to a mother who asked for a communication from her deceased daughter: "Then the turning table heads toward the unhappy mother writhing in nervous spasms. When the violence of her emotions abate, she is given a copy of her sentence:, *cost twenty francs*; and that does not seem expensive to have words received from an adored girl."

According to the article's author, the seance was not held in such a way as to command respect and inner retreat, for he adds:

"The gentleman who questioned the spirits did not appear to me worthy of the situation or the interlocutors; with a little more ceremony than he would use when cutting a leg of roast beef sticking up from a tavern table."

The most damaging thing is that he was able to say that he saw spirit communications being sold at a price. However we can only pity him for judging an entire work based on a mere parody; which is what most critics do, then saying, "I saw."

These abuses, as I have said, are exceptions, and very rare exceptions at that. If I insist on highlighting it, it is because these are facts that most lend themselves to malicious criticism, when not to the work of calculated malevolence itself. Moreover, they are unable to spread in presence of the immense majority of serious people who understand the true mission of Spiritism and the obligations it imposes. Its essence entails dignity and gravity. It is therefore a duty to decline all solidarity with the abuses that could compromise it, and to let it be known that you would not be their champions either before the courts or before public opinion.

But that's not the only pitfall. I have said that our adversaries have another tactic to achieve their ends, which is to attempt to sow discord among adherents of Spiritism, by fanning the flame of petty passions, jealousy and grudges; by creating schisms; by bringing about causes of antagonism and rivalry among several groups to get them to form divided camps. And do not think that it is our declared enemies that will act in this way; they will be cautious in this respect! They are alleged friends of Spiritism, and often most charming and engaging. Sometimes they will even deftly use true but weak sympathizers of Spiritism as cat's paws to draw the chestnuts from the fire for them, after outwitting them who proceed to act in good faith and without suspicion. Bear in mind that the fight is not over and that the enemy is still at your door. Be constantly on your guard so that they do not take you by surprise and trip you up. In case of uncertainty, you have an unmistakable lighthouse that cannot deceive you, which is *charity*. Therefore, hold as being of suspicious origin, any counsel or insinuation which would tend to sow discord among yourselves, and lead you away from the right path that teaches you charity in all and for all.

11

Spirits form neither a secret society nor an affiliation; they must therefore have no secret sign of recognition; they teach nothing and practice nothing that cannot be known to everyone, and therefore have nothing to hide. A sign, a watchword, might be taken by pretended brothers and sisters, and this would not give you any further advancement.

You already have a watchword that is understood from one end of the world to the other: *charity*. This word is easy for everyone to pronounce, but true charity cannot be faked. By the practice of true charity, you will always recognize a brother or sister, even if they are not Spiritists; and you should extend your hand to them, for if they do not share your beliefs, they will not be less benevolent and tolerant toward you.

A secret sign of recognition is even less necessary today as Spiritism is no longer in hiding. For those who do not have the courage of expressing their opinion, it would be useless, for they would not use it. As for others, they are recognized simply for speaking without fear.

III

SOME PEOPLE SEE SPIRITISM AS A DANGER TO
UNENLIGHTENED CLASSES, WHO, NOT BEING ABLE TO
UNDERSTAND IT IN ITS PURE ESSENCE, MIGHT DISTORT ITS
TENETS, DEGENERATING IT INTO SUPERSTITION.
WHAT TO ANSWER THEM?

The same could be said of the most useful things, and if it were necessary to remove everything that could be misused, I do not know what would remain, starting with the printing press which can be used to disseminate pernicious doctrines; not to mention reading, writing, etc. One could even ask God why It gave language to certain people. We abuse everything, even the most holy things. If Spiritism had originated in the ignorant classes, there is no doubt that many superstitions would have made their way into it, but it was born in the enlightened classes, and it is only after having been polished and purified that it now enters the less enlightened classes, where it arrives freed by experience and observation from any bad alloys. What would be really dangerous for the common people is charlatanism; therefore, too much care can not be taken to combat exploitation – this inevitable source of abuse – by every possible means.

We are no longer at the time of begging for light, when it was often said: this is good for the chosen ones, whereas that is good for the others. Light enters the humble workshop and the squalid hut, as the sun of intelligence rises on the horizon and darts fiery rays everywhere. Spiritist ideas follow this movement; they are in the air, and it is impossible for anyone to stop them; what is needed is to direct the course. The most important point of Spiritism is its moral aspect: this is what we must endeavor to make understood; and it is remarkable that it is thus that it is generally envisaged now, even in the least enlightened classes; hence its moralizing effect is evident. The following is just an example among thousands:

In a group I attended during my stay in Lyon, a man in a worker's outfit stood up in the back of the room and said, "Sir, six months ago I did not believe in God, the devil, or that I had a soul; I was convinced that when we died, everything died. I did not fear God, since I did not believe in It; I did not fear future troubles, since, in my thinking, everything ended with life. All this is to say that I did not pray, because, since my First Communion, I do not think to have ever set foot in a church again. Moreover I was violent and out of control; in short, I feared nothing, *not even human justice*. Six months ago I was still like that. Then Spiritism came into my life. For two months I struggled; but I read, I understood, and I could not reject the evidence. A true revolution has taken place in me; today I am no longer the same person: I pray every day, and I go to church. As for my character, ask my fellow mates if I changed! Formerly, I was irritated with everything and everybody, the smallest of things made me lose my temper. Now I feel quiet and happy, and thank God for having sent me the light,"

Do you understand what a person who has reached the point of no longer fearing even human justice is capable of doing? Can anyone deny the salutary effect of Spiritism in this case? And there are thousands like him. Illiterate as he was, his understanding of it was no less complete. This happens because Spiritism is not an abstract theory which addresses only the learned and educated. It speaks to the heart, and to understand the language of the heart, there is no need of a diploma. Make it enter in this way a wealthy or a poor abode and it will work wonders.

IV

SINCE SPIRITISM MAKES PEOPLE BETTER AND LEADS THOSE WHO DO NOT BELIEVE IN GOD, IN THE SOUL, AND IN FUTURE LIFE TO BELIEVE IN THEM, IT DOES NOTHING BUT GOOD. SO WHY DOES IT HAVE ENEMIES, AND WHY THOSE WHO DO NOT BELIEVE IN IT DO NOT JUST LEAVE IT ALONE?

Like any new idea, Spiritism has enemies. An idea which would establish itself without any opposition would be a miraculous feat. The more it is false and absurd, the less opponents it will find; whereas it will meet more opponents especially as it proves to be truer and truer, fairer and more useful. This is a natural consequence of the current state of humanity. Every new idea necessarily supplants an old idea; if it is false, ridiculous or impracticable, no one cares about it, because, instinctively, we understand that it has no vitality, and let it die a quiet death. Conversely, if it is fair and fruitful, it frightens those who, in some capacity, pride themselves on their position or material gains, are interested in maintaining the old order, and therefore will fight it all the more fiercely the more formidable it appears to them. Check history, industry, sciences, religions, everywhere you will find the application of this principle. But history also tells us that against absolute truth nothing can prevail; it is established whether one likes it or not, when people are ripe to accept it. It is necessary then that its adversaries conspire against it, since they cannot do otherwise; and, oddly enough, they often boast of having been the first to have such an idea.

One can generally judge the importance of something by the opposition it arouses. Suppose that, entering an unknown country, you learn that one is preparing to repel the enemy who wants to invade them: if you send only four soldiers and a corporal to the frontier, you might think that the enemy is not quite formidable. Now, it would be quite different if you saw a great many battalions with all the paraphernalia of war. So are new ideas. Issue a frankly ridiculous system unable of affecting the greatest interests of society, and no one will even think of fighting it. If, on the contrary, such a system is based on logic and common sense, recruiting many adherents, with clever people being moved by it, then all who live on the old order of things will raise the most formidable batteries against it. Such is the history of Spiritism; those who fight it most fiercely, do not do it out of a misconception, because then one would wonder why they let so many other ideas pass without saying a thing. They do it because it scares them; but we cannot be afraid of gnats, even if sometimes a gnat can shatter a lion.

Notice that, due to a providential wisdom in all things, a new idea of a certain importance never bursts forth suddenly in all its might: it grows up, and gradually pervades habits. In the same way, Spiritism can be called, without presumption, the capital idea of the nineteenth century; and we shall see later on if we have deceived ourselves. Starting with the innocent phenomenon of the turning tables, an infant with which its toughest adversaries played; and penetrating everywhere as an amusement; nonetheless grew up quickly. Today it has reached maturity and has taken its place in the philosophical world. People can no longer play with it. Instead they discuss it and fight it. If it had been a lie, a utopia, it would not have grown out of its swaddling clothes.

V

IF CRITICISM DID NOT PREVENT SPIRITISM FROM ADVANCING, WOULD ITS PROGRESS NOT BE EVEN FASTER IF IT HAD KEPT SILENT?

To advance faster would be difficult. I think that it would, on the contrary, advance less, because criticism would pummel a double-bass drum against it. In advancing despite the attacks, it proved its own strength, since it walked relying only on itself, and having as weapon only the power of an idea. Does a soldier who reaches the top of a redoubt through a hail of bullets not have more merit than the one before whom the enemies open their ranks to let him pass? By opposing it, the adversaries of Spiritism give it the prestige of struggle and victory.

VI

EVEN MORE HARMFUL TO SPIRITISM THAN THE PASSIONATE ATTACKS OF ITS ENEMIES, IS WHAT SO-CALLED FOLLOWERS PUBLISH UNDER ITS NAME. CERTAIN PUBLICATIONS ARE OBVIOUSLY REGRETTABLE, BECAUSE THEY CAN ONLY GIVE A WRONG IDEA AND LEND THEMSELVES TO RIDICULE. ONE WONDERS WHY GOD WOULD ALLOW SUCH THINGS TO HAPPEN AND NOT IMPART THE SAME LIGHT UNTO EVERYONE. IS THERE ANY WAY TO REMEDY THIS INCONVENIENCE, WHICH SEEMS TO US ONE OF THE MAJOR PITFALLS OF SPIRITISM?

This is a very serious question that requires some development. I will first say that it is not the first time that a new idea, especially one holding some importance, meets with obstacles. Was not Christianity itself struck in the head as an imposture? Amidst its early apostles; and even among its own disseminators, can we not find enfants terribles who embarrassed the cause? Why, then, should Spiritism be privileged?

I would also like to add that what may seem an evil to you is ultimately something good. To understand it, one must not look only at the present, one must above all see the future. Humankind is afflicted with many evils that eat away at it and have their source in pride and selfishness. Do you hope to cure it instantly? Do you believe that these passions which reign supreme can be easily dethroned? No; they raise their heads to bite those who come to disturb their peace. Undoubtedly this is the cause of certain oppositions: the moral values of Spiritism is not suitable for everybody; not daring to attack such values, they attack their source.

Although Spiritism has undoubtedly produced veritable miracles of moral reform, to think that such a transformation can be sudden and universal would indicate a lack of knowledge regarding humanity. Among its followers there are some who, as I have said, see Spiritism only on the surface, and do not understand its essential goal. Either for misplaced pride or lack of judgment, they accept only that which flatters them, while repelling whatever might diminish them. Therefore it is not surprising that some Spiritists interpret it the wrong way. This may be unfortunate for the time being, but I say that it is of no consequence to the future.

You ask why God does not prevent mistakes? Ask God, then, why It did not create perfect beings all at once, instead of giving them the trouble and merit of perfecting themselves, Why It did not give birth to the child as an adult being, reasonable and enlightened instead of letting the newborn acquire experience from life. Why does the tree reach its full growth only after many years, and the fruit achieves maturity only when the right season has come? Ask God why Christianity, which is Its law and work, has undergone so many fluctuations since its origin; why did It allow humans to use Its sacred name to commit so many abuses, even crimes, and shed so much blood? Nothing is done all of a sudden in Nature; everything progresses gradually according to the Creator's immutable laws, and these laws always lead to the goal which It has proposed to Itself. Yet humanity on Earth is still young, despite the pretension of its doctors and savants. Spiritism, too, is barely born; it is growing up quickly, as you can see, and it is in good health; but give it time to reach adulthood. Moreover, I have said that the differences of which you complain have their good side; it is the spirits themselves who come to explain it. Here is a passage from a spirit communication given on this subject:

"Enlightened Spiritists should congratulate themselves on the fact that false and contradictory ideas were exposed at the very beginning, because they got ruined, having been fought and eliminated during the period of infancy of Spiritism. Once purged of all these bad things, it will only shine with a brighter light, taking it a step closer to reaching its full-fledged development."

To this judicious appreciation, I would add that Spiritism is like a child who at first sows its wild oats, and then, afterwards, becomes well-behaved. But to judge the effect of these discordances, it suffices to observe what is taking place. What are they relying on? On individual opinions that can rally a few people, because there is no idea, no matter how absurd, that will not find supporters; however one can gauge its value by the preponderance it acquires. Now, where can you see those individuals acquiring any relevance? Where do you see them making school, threatening by the number of their adherents the cause you now embrace? Nowhere. Far from it, divergent ideas are incessantly seeing their partisans shrink in number to join the ranks of the unity which is law for the immense majority, if not the unanimity rule. Of all the systems hatched from the very beginning of spirit manifestations, how many still remain standing? Among these systems there is one which, in a certain city, had taken, a few years ago, fairly large proportions – now count its members today. Do you believe that, had it been right, it would not have grown up and absorbed its competitors? In such a case, the number of supporters is a clue that can leave no doubt. As for me, I declare that if the philosophical doctrine of which I made myself the disseminator were repulsed unanimously; if, instead of growing up, I had seen it decline; if another more rational theory had gained more sympathy and had peremptorily demonstrated that I was in error; I would then consider it to be a proud foolishness to dwell on a false idea, because, first and foremost, truth cannot be a matter of anyone's choice, or of self-esteem, and

I would be the first to say to you: "My fellow beings, behold the light and follow it; this is the example I am giving you now."

Moreover, error almost always carries with it its antidote, and it cannot prevail eternally. Sooner or later, blinded by some ephemeral successes, it is seized by a sort of vertigo, throwing itself into aberrations that soon precipitate its fall. This applies both to big and small. You deplore the eccentricities of certain writings published under the mantle of Spiritism. You should instead bless them, for it is by their very excesses that error meets its demise. What struck you in these writings? What has been a cause of repulsion for you, and has often prevented you from finishing reading it, if not contents that have violently hurt your common sense? If the falsity of ideas had not been so obvious, so shocking, perhaps you would not have noticed it; and perhaps you would even have let it pass, whereas you are certainly struck by glaring errors which act as antivenin.

These errors often come from irresponsible spirits, and spirits that pose as systematizers or false scholars pleasing themselves with publishing their fantasies and utopias through people they have managed to outwit to the point of making them accept with eyes shut everything they are offered in a few grains of wheat mixed with the chaff of lies. But since these spirits possess neither true knowledge nor real wisdom, they cannot sustain their farce for long, and their ignorance eventually betrays them. God allows that such communications let slip so many gross errors, and things that are so absurd and even ridiculous, with ideas which even the most basic notions of science prove to be eminently false, so that they end up killing both the false system and the book that conveys it.

Undoubtedly it would be better if only good quality material were published, but since it is otherwise, do not fear the influence of these works in the future. Although they can momentarily produce a flash in the pan, when they fail to rely on rigorous logic, after a few years, frequently even after a few months, see what is left of them. In such cases, booksellers have an infallible thermometer.

Which leads me to the subject of the publication of mediumistic messages.

As much as such publications can be useful if they are made with discernment, they can be also harmful when done otherwise. Among the spirit messages, there are some which, good as they may be, only interest the one who obtained them, and offer other readers only banalities. Other messages are of interest only in the circumstances in which they were given, and without knowing such circumstances they become insignificant. This would only be inconvenient for the publisher's income; but there are some of communications that are bad both in substance and in style, and which, being apocryphally signed by respectable names, contain absurd or trivial statements, which naturally lend themselves to ridicule and give rise to criticism. It is even worse when, under the cloak of such illustrious names, they formulate bizarre systems or crude scientific heresies. There would be no inconvenience in publishing this sort of communications if they were accompanied by comments, either refuting the errors, or reminding that they are the expression of an individual opinion for which one does not take any responsibility. They might even contain an instructive side by showing the degree of aberration of the ideas that certain spirits can embrace. Yet the disadvantage lies in purely and simply publishing them, thus presenting them as the expression of truth, and subscribing to the authenticity of signatures of which common sense cannot admit. As spirits have free will and their own opinion of humans and things, it will be understood that one's prudence and sense of propriety are required in selecting them. In the interest of Spiritism, it is therefore necessary to make a very severe choice in such situations, and to carefully exclude anything that may, for any reason, produce a bad impression. While a medium who, by complying with this rule, could make a very informative collection which would then be read with interest, conversely, by publishing all that he/she obtains without any method or discernment, would end up making several detestable volumes whose least inconvenience would be the fact of not being read.

We must be aware that if serious Spiritism supports with joy and eagerness any book done under proper conditions, from whatever source it comes, it also repudiates any eccentric publications. All Spiritists who are concerned that its tenets are not compromised must therefore hasten to disavow such books, especially since, if some might be written in good faith, others may be even conceived by enemies of Spiritism, with the purpose of discrediting it and being able to justify accusations against it. That is why, I repeat, it is necessary that one knows what one accepts and what one rejects.

VII

IN PRESENCE OF THE WISE TEACHINGS OFFERED BY THE SPIRITS, AND THE GREAT NUMBER OF PEOPLE WHO ARE BROUGHT BACK TO GOD BY THEIR COUNSELING, HOW CAN ONE POSSIBLY BELIEVE THAT THIS IS THE WORK OF THE DEVIL?

The devil would be very awkward in this case, for who can it subjugate better than those who believe neither in God, nor in their own souls, nor in a future life? And to whom can it therefore make all that it wishes to do? Is it possible to be more out of the Church than one who believes in nothing, even if he/she was baptized? The devil needs do nothing to attract such individuals, and it would be foolish for the devil to bring them back to God, to prayer and to all beliefs that can divert one from evil, so as to have fun by making them plunge back again. Such a conception gives a very poor idea of the devil, which is usually represented as being extremely cunning, by making it very little fearsome instead. The man in Aesop's fable "The Fisherman and the Little Fish,"[13] reminds us of the expected common sense. What to say of someone who, having a bird in a cage, would set it free only to try to catch it again one moment later? This is not sustainable. But there is another, more serious explanation.

If only the devil could manifest itself, it would be either with or without God's permission. If it did it without God's permission, that would mean that it is more powerful than God. Now, if it would be with God's permission, that would mean that God is not good, since giving to the spirit of evil, to the exclusion of all others, the power to seduce humans, without allowing good spirits to come and fight against such an influence, could not possibly be an act of goodness or justice. It would be even worse if, according to the opinion of certain persons, the fate of all human beings would be irrevocably fixed after death, for then God would be voluntarily and knowingly hastening Its created beings into eternal torment, by making them trapped by pitfalls. One cannot conceive of God without the infinity of all Its attributes; to cut off or

---

13 [Trans. note] "O Sir, what good can I be to you, and how little am I worth? I am not yet come to my full size. Pray spare my life, and put me back into the sea. I shall soon become a large fish fit for the tables of the rich; and then you can catch me again, and make a handsome profit of me." The fisherman replied: *"I should be a very simple fellow, if I were to forego my certain gain for an uncertain profit."* AESOP, *Three Hundred and Fifty Aesop's Fables* (Trans. G. F. Townsend. London: Routledge, 1867).

diminish a single one of them would be the negation of God, since that would imply the possibility of a more perfect being. This philosophical doctrine refutes itself, therefore finding too little credit even among the indifferent, to deserve any further consideration. Its time will soon be gone, and those who advocate it will willingly abandon it when they realize that it harms more than it helps them.

VIII

WHAT TO THINK OF MOSES' PROHIBITION IMPOSED ON HEBREWS OF EVOKING THE SOULS OF THE DEAD? WHAT ARE ITS CONSEQUENCE FOR CURRENT EVOCATIONS?

The first consequence of this is that it is indeed possible to evoke the souls of the dead and to converse with them, since any prohibition of doing something implies the possibility of doing it. Would it be necessary, for example, to make a law prohibiting one from going the Moon?[14]

It is really odd to see the enemies of Spiritism claim from the past whatever they think that can serve their arguments, while repudiating the past whenever it does not suit them. Since they invoke the Laws of Moses in this circumstance, why do they not claim their application for everyone and everything? I doubt, however, that any of them would be tempted to revive Mose's code, and especially his draconian penal code,

---

14 [Trans. note] In the mid-19th century, a complete impossibility.

so lavish with the application of the death penalty. Is it then that they would find that Moses was right in some cases and wrong in others? But then, why would he have been right about the evocations? It is, they say, that Moses made laws appropriate to his time and to the ignorant and intractable people he led; yet such laws, good at the time, are no longer in keeping with our customs and our enlightenment. This is precisely what we say about the prohibition of evocations. To do it, he must have had a motive, which was as follows:

The Hebrews, while in the desert, greatly regretted leaving behind the pleasant amenities of Egypt, and that was the cause of their incessant revolts, which Moses could often repress only through extermination; hence the excessive severity of his laws. In such state of affairs, he had to strive to breaking any links his people might still retain with habits and customs which could remind them of Egypt. Yet one of the usages that the Hebrews had brought with them was that of spirit evocations, practiced in that country since time immemorial. There is more: this usage, which seems to have been well understood and wisely practiced by the few initiates to the mysteries, had degenerated into abuse and superstition in the populace, who saw it as an art of divination, which was exploited, no doubt, by charlatans, just as fortune tellers do today. The Hebrew people, ignorant and rude, had taken only the abusive practice. With his prohibition, Moses acted both politically and wisely. Today, things are not the same, and what could be a disadvantage then is no longer so in the current state of society. But we, too, rise up against the abuse that might be made of communications beyond the grave, and we say that it is indeed sacrilegious, not to talk to the souls of those who have departed, but to do it irresponsibly, irreverently, or in hope of financial gain. That is why true Spiritism repudiates all that could deprive these relations of their deeply serious and religious character, because it would be a true profanation. As souls can communicate, this happens only with God's permission, and there can be no harm in doing what God allows. Evil, in this as in all things, lies in its abuse and misuse.

IX

HOW CAN THIS PASSAGE OF THE GOSPEL BE EXPLAINED:
"FOR FALSE CHRISTS AND FALSE PROPHETS WILL ARISE AND
PERFORM GREAT SIGNS AND WONDERS, SO AS TO LEAD
ASTRAY, IF POSSIBLE, EVEN THE ELECT."[15]
DETRACTORS OF SPIRITISM TURN IT INTO A WEAPON
AGAINST SPIRITISTS AND MEDIUMS.

If one would note in the Gospel all the words which are used as condemnation by the opponents of Spiritism, one could fill a volume with them. Therefore it is at least foolhardy of them to raise a question that can fire back at them, which is even better, as it is to the benefit of Spiritism.

---

15 [Trans. note] Matthew 24:24.

First of all, neither Spiritists nor mediums pass themselves off as Christs or prophets; they declare that they do not perform miracles to strike the senses, and that all the tangible phenomena which occur by their influence are effects within the laws of Nature, which cannot be construed as miracles. Therefore if they had wished to encroach on the privileges of prophets, they would not have been so careful in depriving themselves of the most powerful prestige: the gift of miracles. By giving the explanation of those phenomena which, without it, might have been considered super-natural in the eyes of the populace, they kill the false ambition which might have become an exploitation for profit.

Now let us suppose that an individual claims to have the attributes of a prophet; it is not by doing what mediums do that he/she will prove it, and no enlightened Spiritists will allow themselves to be caught by such a foolish bait. For this reason, Mr. Home,[16] in case he had been a charlatan and a greedy individual, could have put on airs of being a heavenly envoy. What is the character of a true prophet? A true prophet is an envoy of God to warn or enlighten humanity. Now, an envoy of God can only be a higher-order spirit and, as a human being, a good individual. He/she will be recognized through their actions, which will bear the imprint of their superiority, and the great things they

---

16 [Trans. note] Famous Scottish medium D. D. Home (1833–1866).

will do *for the cause of good and by means of good*, which will reveal their mission especially to future generations. Because this often leads him/her to be unwittingly guided by a superior power, and almost always to the detriment of their own personal wellbeing. Therefore it is not the individual that will give himself/ herself the title of being a prophet: it is his/her fellow beings that will recognize him/her as such, most often after the latter has died

If, then, an individual had the pretension to be the reincarnation of this or that prophet, he/she would have to prove it by the excellence of his/her moral qualities, which *in no respect* can be lesser than the ones associated with the illustrious name he/she now wishes to impersonate. Yet this role is neither easy to sustain nor very pleasant, for it can often impose painful hardships and heavy sacrifices, even of one's own life. Right now, there are in the world several pretended Elijahs, Jeremiases and Ezekiels, among others, who would not cope very well with life in the desert, but find it very convenient to live at the expense of their deluded followers, because of the illustrious name they borrowed. There are even several Christs, as there were several kings Louis 17th, who all notably lack charity, self-denial, humility, and eminent moral superiority – in a word, all the virtues of Christ. If, like Jesus Christ, they had nowhere to lay their heads, and if they had a cross before their eyes, they would soon abdicate a kingship so unprofitable in this world. Through his/

her work, we recognize the worker. Those who wish to place themselves above humanity, are only worthy if they do not wish to have the fate of the jay decked with the feathers of the peacock, or the donkey clothed with the skin of the lion. A humiliating fall awaits them in this world, and a more terrible disappointment in the afterlife, for it is there that whoever rises will be humbled.

Suppose now that some individual endowed with great mediumistic or magnetic power wants to claim for himself/herself the title of prophet or of Christ. He/she *will perform great signs and wonders, so as to lead astray even the elect*, that is to say, a few good persons of good faith. Such an individual may have the appearance, but will he/she have the *virtues*? Because there lies the genuine touchstone.

Thus Spiritism also says: Beware of false prophets! And it has come to tear off their mask. It must be known that it repudiates all sorts of trickery; and will not cover with its mantle any abuse that might be perpetrated in its name.

X

GUIDELINES ON FORMING SPIRITIST GROUPS AND SOCIETIES

I was often asked in several places for advice on group formation. I have little to say in this respect, so if one would like to refer to the instructions contained in *The Mediums' Book*; I will now add only a few words.

The first condition should be to form a core of serious persons, however small it may be. If it were only five or six members, provided they were enlightened, sincere, imbued with Spiritist tenets and united in intention, that would be a hundred times better than introducing curious and indifferent people into the group. These founding members should then establish a regulation that will function as a rule for new members.

This regulation should be very simple and involve only the matters of internal discipline, for it does not require the same details as for a large and regularly constituted society. Each group can therefore set it up as it sees fit. However, for ease of use and consistency, I will provide a model that can be adapted according to circumstances and local needs. In any case, the essential goal that must be proposed to the participants is their inner retreat, the maintenance of order, and to discard any person that is not animated by serious intentions and could be a cause of trouble; that is why one cannot be too scrupulous when screening new members for introduction into the group. Do not be afraid that such severity might harm the spread of Spiritism. On the contrary, serious meetings are those which make the most proselytes; whereas frivolous meetings, that is, those which are not held with order and dignity, and where curious newcomers may come to vent their jokes, inspire neither attention nor respect – and un-believers come out even less convinced than they were on entering. These latter meetings are the joy of the enemies of Spiritism, while the former ones are their nightmare; and I know people who would willingly multiply the frivolous ones, provided the serious ones were annihilated as a result. Unfortunately for them, the opposite has been happening. One should also bear in mind that the desire to be admitted increases because of the difficulty in doing so. As for any actual dissemination, it is much less accomplished by the number of attendees that a meeting or two can hardly convince, than by a preliminary study, and by the behavior of group members outside the meetings.

To exclude women[17] would be an insult to their discernment, which, without flattery, can sometimes provide key points to those offered by certain men, or even certain literary critics. Their presence commands a more rigorous observation of the laws of urbanity, and curbs the complacent, easy-going attitude of meetings exclusively composed of men. Why would one deprive them of the moralizing influence of Spiritism? A sincere female Spiritist can only be a good woman, a good wife and a good mother. Because of her very position, she often needs more than most individuals the sublime consolations of Spiritism. She will be stronger and more resigned in life trials. Moreover, do we not know that spirits have a gender only for the duration of an incarnation? If the equality of women's rights

---

17 [Trans. note] In the mid-19th century, women did not have the right to vote in public elections. Some individuals even doubted that they had souls (sic!). Kardec stood firmly against such notorious prejudices.

is to be recognized somewhere, it must certainly be among Spiritists, and the propagation of Spiritism will infallibly hasten the abolition of the privileges that men have arrogated to themselves through the law of the strongest. The advent of Spiritism will mark an era of legal emancipation for women.

Do not be afraid to admit young men into your groups either. The gravity of the meeting will reflect upon their character; they will become more serious; and draw early from the teachings of good spirits this living faith in God and in the future, this feeling of duty toward one's family, which make one more obliging and respectful, while also tempering the effervescence of passions.

As for the legal formalities, there is none required in France for meetings that do not exceed twenty people. Beyond this number, regular and periodic meetings must get an authorization, unless there is a tolerance which should not be taken for granted as a right, but has been enjoyed by most Spiritist groups, because of their peaceful, exclusively moral character, and because they do not constitute associations or affiliations. In any case, Spiritists must be the first to give the example of compliance to the laws and regulations, whenever required.

Lately, some special purposes groups have been formed, whose multiplication I most emphatically encourage. These could be called *study groups*. There is little or no discussion in them, except reading and explaining *The Spirits' Book, The Mediums' Book,* and articles published in *The Spiritist Review*. Some devoted people gather a number of listeners for this purpose in order to make up for the difficulty of reading and studying on their own. I wholeheartedly applaud this initiative which I hope will be emulated by others, and which cannot fail to yield the most successful results. There is no need for one to be an orator or teacher; it is a family reading, followed by some explanations without pretension to eloquence and within the reach of everyone.

Whether they are special purposes groups or not, many have the habit of opening their seances by reading some passages from *The Spirits' Book* or *The Mediums' Book*.[18] I would be glad to see all groups adopt this practice, whose effect is to draw one's attention to the principles that we might have misunderstood or lost sight of. In this case, it is useful for group directors or presidents to select in advance the passages that will be read, in order to match this choice to the circumstances.

There is no wrong in recommending these books as the basis of study, since they are the only ones where science is developed in all their parts and in a methodical manner; but it would be mistaken to think that I claim my books to be the only source, to the point of excluding others, many of which certainly deserve the

---

18 [Trans. note] In 1862, A. KARDEC had not yet published *The Gospel according to Spiritism* and the remaining books of the Codification.

sympathy of all good Spiritists. In a thorough study, moreover, everything must be examined, even the bad ones. I therefore consider it very useful to read the criticisms to highlight their emptiness and lack of logic. There is certainly not a single one of them that would be able to shake the faith of any sincere Spiritist. Such criticisms can only strengthen it, since they have often given rise to Spiritism among unbelievers, who have taken the trouble to check it out. The same applies to certain books which, although made with a serious purpose, contain no less blatant errors or eccentricities which one does well in pointing out.

Now here is another practice whose adoption would be no less useful. It is essential that each group collects and transcribes the spirit communications it receives, so that they can easily be referred to when needed. Seeing their instructions being neglected, spirits would soon grow weary. Furthermore, it is particularly necessary to make a special, very clear and clean collection of the most beautiful and instructive communications, and to reread some of them at each seance, in order to put them to good use.

XI

ON THE USE OF EXTERNAL SIGNS OF WORSHIP IN GROUPS

I have also been asked several times if it is useful to start the seances with prayers and external religious acts. My answer is not only from me, but also from eminent spirits that have addressed this issue.

There can be no doubt that it is not only useful, but necessary to call, by means of a special invocation, a prayer of sorts, for the aid of good spirits. This can only be achieved by retreating inside ourselves, an essential prerequisite in any serious meetings. The same cannot be said of outward signs of worship, with which some groups think they ought to open their seances, and which have more than one inconvenience, in spite of the good intention they may suggest to one's thought.

Everything in the meetings must be religious, that is, performed with seriousness, respect, and meditation; but we must not forget that Spiritism is addressed to all religious systems; therefore, it should not mime the forms and uses of any one in particular. Its enemies are already too bent presenting it as a new sect to be offered another excuse to fight it. Therefore we must not accredit this opinion by the use of formulas which opponents would not fail to pinpoint, accusing Spiritist meetings of being assemblies of religionists and schismatic rebels – for, make no mistake, these formulas are not likely to win over any antagonists. Spiritism, by calling people of all beliefs to bring them under the banner of charity and loving fellowship; by getting them used to the idea of seeing one another as brothers and sisters, regardless of their way of worshiping God; should not offend anyone's religious convictions by the use of any kind of external signs of worship. There are few Spiritist meetings of any kind, especially in France, where members or participants do not belong to different religions. If Spiritism placed itself openly on the terrain of one of them, it would dismiss the others. Now, as there are Spiritists coming from all religious denominations, we would see the formation of Catholic, Jewish or Protestant groups, and thus perpetuate the religious antagonism that Spiritism should abolish.

This is also the reason why we must refrain, in meetings, from discussing particular dogmas, which would inexplicably offend certain consciences, whereas issues of moral conduct are shared by all religions in all countries. Spiritism is a neutral ground on which all religious opinions can meet and join hands; however, conflict could arise from controversy. Do not forget that conflict is one of the means by which the enemies of Spiritism seek to attack it; it is with this purpose in mind that they often push certain groups to deal with annoying or compromising issues, under the specious pretext that we should not put the light under a bushel. Do not get caught up in this trap, and may group directors stand firm to reject any suggestion of this kind, if they do not want to be associated as accessories to such maneuvers.

The use of external signs of worship would have the same effect, causing a split among Spiritism adherents. Some would eventually conclude that we do not do enough, and others that we do too much. To avoid this inconvenience, which is a very serious one, it is advisable to abstain from all liturgical prayer, not excepting the Lord's Prayer, however beautiful it may be. On entering into a Spiritist meeting, no one abjures his/her religion, and each one says, by themselves and mentally, all the prayers that he/she deems appropriate, nothing more, and we all engage in it. But never ostensibly and especially never as an official practice. The same applies to doing signs of the cross, to kneeling, and other gestures; otherwise, there would be no reason to prevent a Muslim Spiritist, participating in a group, from prostrating the face to the ground and reciting aloud the sacramental formula, "There is no other god but God and Muhammad is His prophet."

There is no inconvenience when prayers said for any purpose are independent of any particular worship. Following this line of thought, I think it superfluous to point out what would be ridiculous to repeat in chorus, by all in the audience, any liturgical prayer or formula of any kind, as reported in some places.

It should be understood that what has just been said applies only to groups or societies formed of persons unknown to one another, but does not concern intimate family meetings, where each member is naturally free to do as he/she pleases, because in such case nobody will feel offended.

DRAFT REGULATIONS

TO BE USED BY SPIRITIST GROUPS
AND SMALL SPIRITIST SOCIETIES

PROPOSED BY THE PARISIAN SOCIETY OF SPIRITIST STUDIES
IN ORDER TO MAINTAIN A UNITY OF
PRINCIPLES AND ACTIONS[19]

The undersigned, having resolved to form a Spiritist group or society in the city of _____, under the title of _____ group or society, have agreed upon the following provisions, which shall be accepted by any person who may wish to join it later.

1. The purpose of this Society is the study of Spiritist science, mainly with regard to its application to morality and to the knowledge of the invisible world. Political and social economy issues are prohibited as well as any religious controversies.

19 The Parisian Society of Spiritist Studies will gladly welcome reports from groups and societies that wish to inform it about their formation and keep it updated about their progress.

Please refer to A. KARDEC, *The Mediums' Book*, for unabridged draft regulations for large societies, as based on the Parisian Society of Spiritist Studies.

2. This Society declares itself to rally support for the principles formulated in The Spirits' Book and The Mediums' Book.

It places itself under the protection of the Spirit _____, chosen by itself to be its Guide and Spiritual President.

It takes for motto:

Without charity there is no salvation.

Without charity there is no true Spiritist.

3. The number of the Society's accredited members is fixed at ___ (*or:* is unlimited).

To be a member of the Society, one must have given sufficient proof of his/her knowledge of Spiritism and that they are in keeping with its tenets.

The Society will determine the nature and extent of the evidence and warranties to be provided, as well as the manner of presentation and admission.

Anyone who qualifies may be admitted without distinction as to religion or nationality.

The Society will exclude anyone who might bring elements of trouble into meetings, or for any other cause, and thus waste time in unnecessary discussions.

An exact list of all members will be kept, with their address, profession and date of admission.

4. All members owe one another reciprocal benevolence and good behavior; they must, in all circumstances, put the general good above personal matters and self-interest, and act with respect toward one another, according to the principles of charity.

5. When the Society is deemed to have become too numerous, or because of circumstances, it can be divided into various groups according to local needs.

Various groups or societies of the same city, whether spontaneously formed or built around a common area of interest, as they have the same principles and strive for the same goal, must cordially sympathize and fraternize with one another, thus avoiding any cause of disagreement.

NOTE: In case of dissent, the one who thinks he/she is right should prove it through more charity and more kindness. The wrong would obviously be on the side of those who would denigrate the others and throw stones at them.

6. The Society will hold meetings every _____ at ___ a.m./p.m. It will be presided over by a person to be appointed for this purpose, for a fixed time.

The seances held at ____ are reserved exclusively for accredited members, save some exceptions.

At other sittings and seances, outside listeners will be admitted, if the Society sees fit to do so. The admission of unknown persons is subject to conditions that the Society will set. However, it will absolutely refuse entry of anyone who is only attracted by curiosity or who has no prior notions of Spiritism.

7.   Any outside listener or guest must be introduced by one of the members who is held accountable for their presence. Any unknown person who refuses to identify himself/herself will be strictly denied entry.

Seances should never be public; that is to say, in no circumstance should the doors be opened to the first comer.

8.   Since Spiritism aims at a fraternal unity of all religious denominations under the banner of truth, and its groups and societies accept members or participants without distinction of faith or belief, it is forbidden in meetings any form of prayer or liturgical sign belonging to any specific worship. Nonetheless, everyone is free to do in private what his/her conscience prescribes for them.

Note: Everything in the sittings or seances should be religiously serious, yet nothing in them should give the impression of assemblies of a religious denomination.

9.   The order of proceedings in the meetings shall be as follows, except when modifications are required by circumstances:

1st) General invocation, in prayer, to call for the help of good spirits;[20]

2nd) Reading of the minutes and the communications of the preceding meeting duly tidied up;

20 There is no fixed formula. The following are some examples of those used at the Parisian Society of Spiritist Studies:

3RD) Reading and commentary of some passages extracted from *The Spirits' Book* and *The Mediums' Book*, or other books relating to Spiritism;

4TH) Reading of some instructive communications from the collection of the Society, or obtained outside the Society;

5TH) Stories of various facts concerning Spiritism;

6TH) Work of mediums: spontaneous dictations and dissertations chosen by the spirits, or concerning a certain subject, or in answer to proposed questions. Special evocations:

The evocations and the questions to be proposed will, as far as possible, be prepared in advance.

7TH) Thanking the good spirits that manifested themselves during the seance.

10. All spirit communications obtained in the group/ Society are its property and it can dispose of them as it pleases. They should be transcribed and kept for

---

"We pray to Almighty God to send us good spirits to assist us, and to ward off those that might mislead us; give us the necessary light to distinguish the truth from deception."

"Also ward off evil spirits which could sow disunity among us; if some of them attempt to break into here, in the name of God, we adjure them to withdraw."

"Good spirits that deign to come and educate us, make us receptive to your advices;turn us away from all thoughts of selfishness, pride, envy, and jealousy; inspire us with charity, benevolence toward our fellow beings, humility, devotion and self-denial; and make every personal feeling vanish in us when faced with the thought of general good."

"In particular, we pray to the Spirit _____, our Spiritual Guide, to assist and watch over us."

consultation as needed. The mediums who produced them can keep a copy for himself/herself.

A special collection of the most remarkable and instructive communications, properly copied on a book set for this purpose, will be organized, forming a sort of guide or moral memento of the Society, to be read from time to time.

11. The Society's president will intervene in the reading of any communication addressing subject matters that the Society is not supposed to deal with.

12. Silence and inner retreat must be observed during the seances. All futile questions of personal interest, of pure curiosity, or those subjecting spirits to trials, as well as those which have no instructive purpose whatsoever, are entirely forbidden.

Also prohibited are any discussions which might divert from the main objectives, or are extraneous to those embraced by the Society.

Those who wish to speak must ask permission from the president.

13. The Society may, if it deems it advisable, devote special meetings for the instruction of novices, either through verbal explanations or by a regular and methodical reading of the basic books. Only persons with a serious desire to learn and who are registered for this purpose will be admitted. These meetings, as well as the others, will not be open to the first comer, nor will they admit people that have not been introduced beforehand.

14. Any publication relating to Spiritism that emanates from the Society will be reviewed with the utmost care in order to prune anything that would be useless or could produce a bad impression. The members undertake not to publish anything on Spiritism without first seeking advice from the Society.

15. The Society invites all mediums who wish to put their mediumistic faculties at its service, not to make any observations or express criticisms regarding the spirit communications they obtain. Furthermore, the Society would rather dispense with those mediums who believe in the absolute infallibility and in the identity of the spirits that manifest themselves through them.

16. If necessary, to cover administrative expenses of the Society, a membership fee will be established, whose amount, use and mode of payment will be decided by the Society. In this case, it should appoint a treasurer.

It shall be expressly stipulated that this contribution will be paid only by the accredited members of the society, and that in no circumstance, nor in any manner, will any payment be demanded or charged from the audience or occasional guests, by way of entrance fees.

17. The Society may form a charitable or relief fund through membership fees or fund subscriptions collected from any person wishing to participate, regardless of being a member of the Society. The use of these funds will be controlled by a committee which shall report to the Society.

18. Any member who is found to be a constant cause of trouble and tends to sow dissent among other members, as well as anyone who has notoriously fallen into disrepute, and whose conduct or reputation could harm the consideration enjoyed by the Society, may be informally invited to give his/her resignation. In case of refusal, the Society may officially vote it.

A SELECT
BIBLIOGRAPHY

A SELECT BIBLIOGRAPHY

KARDEC, Allan. *Spiritist Prayers*. Trans. H. M. Monteiro. New York: USSF, 2019.

—————. *The Mediums' Book*. Trans. D. W. Kimble, M. M. Saiz. 2nd ed. Brasília, DF (Brazil): ISC/Edicei, 2010.

—————. *The Spirits' Book*. Trans. N. Alves, J. Korngold, H. M. Monteiro. 2nd ed. New York: USSC/USSF, 2016.

—————. *The Spiritist Review (year) 1862*. Trans. L. A. V. Cheim. New York: USSF, 2019.

ALSO BY ALLAN KARDEC
(available from USSF)

KARDEC *The Spiritist Review (year) 1858*. Trans. L. A. V. Cheim. New York: USSC/USSF, 2015.

—————. *The Spiritist Review (year) 1859*. Trans. L. A. V. Cheim. New York: USSC/USSF, 2015.

—————. *The Spiritist Review (year) 1860*. Trans. L. A. V. Cheim. New York: USSC/USSF, 2019.

—————. *The Spiritist Review (year) 1861*. Trans. L. A. V. Cheim. New York: USSC/USSF, 2019.

Book portal: https://is.gd/ussf1

*All **USSF** paperback books with their Kindle® counterparts*
are readily available worldwide
from Amazon®

———————————

Browse USSF book portal: **https://is.gd/ussf1**

✝ *Facsimile of the original French edition title page* ✝

ALLAN KARDEC

VOYAGE SPIRITE

EN 1862

CONTENANT :

1. Les Observations sur l'état du Spiritisme.
2. Les Instructions données dans les différents Groupes.
3. Les instructions sur la formation des Groupes et Sociétés, et un modèle de Règlement à leur usage.

PARIS

CHEZ LES ÉDITEURS DU *LIVRE DES ESPRITS*

35, QUAI DES GRANDS-AUGUSTINS.

LEDOYEN, LIBRAIRE-ÉDITEUR, | AU BUREAU DE LA *REVUE SPIRITE*,
Palais-Royal, 31, galerie d'Orléans. | 59, rue et passage Sainte-Anne.

—

1862

TRADUCTION AUTORISÉE.

**UNITED STATES
SPIRITIST FEDERATION**
New York – USA